SuZy's

LITE

STITCHES

by SuZy Murphy

The canvas on the cover is by Liz at Tapestry Tent.
Stitched by SuZy Murphy with stitch suggestions from Brenda Hart.

ISBN #0-9701330-3-0

Books by SuZy Murphy
SUZY'S SMALL STITCHES
SUZY'S DARN STITCHES
SUZY'S SURPRIZE STITCHES

This book is dedicated to the memory of
J. Jeffrey Gribb, M.D.
June 11, 1962 - May 25, 2002

Jeff, you left us too soon, but you left us with so much. Your impish grin, twinkling eyes and zest for life will always remain with those who love you. I am blessed to be one of them.

Jill,

Jeff's great love. You are an incredible woman and I become prouder of you all the time.

Paige and Parker,

The apples of your Daddy's eye. You are a credit to his memory.

I love you all,
Aunt SuZy

A special thanks to:
Kitty Moeller, Connie Wise, and Penny Franz for stitching models.
Kay Barnes, John Schatteles, and Randy Murphy for proofreading.
Rainbow gallery for supplying Elegance, Subtlety and Petite Treasure Braid for the Stitch Models.
Tapestry Tent, Lees Needle Arts, Sharon Garmize, DeDe Ogden, Sandra Maag Reddell, and
        A Collection of Designs for the use of their designs.

INTRODUCTION

Lite Stitches, called Shadow Stitching by DeDe Ogden, could also be called Open Stitches. They let the canvas show through.

This method can be very effective for a painted canvas that is highly shaded. Handpainted canvases are expensive and works of art by themselves. We buy the canvas and proceed to cover the paint. With Lite Stitches, we cover the canvas with thread, while still letting the artist do all the work. This technique is especially effective for canvases with a great deal of shading and perspective.

The objective is to make the finished piece as true to the artist's original as possible. One way to achieve this is to use a stitch that does not give complete coverage. There are many such stitches in this book.

Another method is to use a fine thread and a regular stitch, such as Brick or Cashmere. The canvas will show through the stitches, but will still be covered. The color photos of the stitched pieces were all done with both lite stitches and a thread that gave lite coverage.

In addition Lite Stitches are great ideas for backgrounds. The Effects Index does not list backgrounds because all the stitches will work for backgrounds. An added benefit is that most of these stitches work up quickly.

CREATING NEW STITCHES FROM OLD FAVORITES:

Still another way of creating open stitches is to rearrange the units of existing stitches. The following chart shows a few of the many different ways Cashmere Stitch can be modified to create new stitches. The Fish by Sharon Garmize was worked with variations of the Cashmere Stitch.

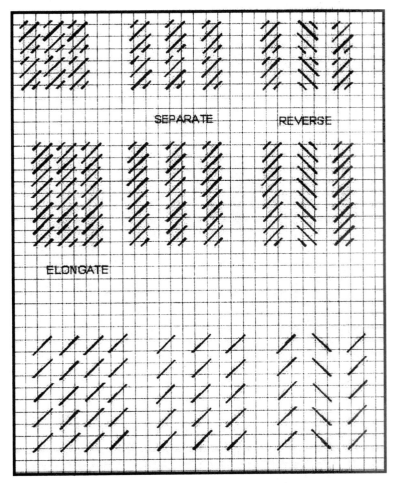

ANCHORING THREADS

Anchoring can be 'tricky' when you have so much open canvas. An away waste knot is possibly the best anchoring technique. Place a knot on the top of the canvas away from where you will be stitching. When you have finished stitching, cut the knot, rethread the needle and weave the thread under the stitches in place. (Be sure to leave a long enough length of thread to be able to put the thread back through the eye of the needle - at least 2 times the length of the needle.)

A pinhead stitch is another suggestion. This is done by placing a knot on the front of the canvas. Then in the area you will be stitching, place a back stitch. Cover a horizontal or vertical thread, not an intersection. The thread can be ended the same way. If more security is needed, work two of these pinhead stitches. Just be sure they will be covered by the stitching and not left showing.

The tails can also be woven under the existing threads on the back. You may want to go through several threads and then go back through the last two one more time. This approach is similar to a back stitch.

You can also weave back and forth through the stitches on the back, going around each one two or three times.

A Securing L can also be used, however, care must be taken, so the L is covered.

THREADS TO USE

Instead of adding strands, fewer threads is the called for approach. One strand of silk or floss worked in Basketweave will show an amazing amount of paint.

Other threads that are fine for 18 mesh canvas are:

Rainbow Gallery - Nordic Gold, Subtlety, Petite Treasure Braid

Kreinik - #4 Braid, Blending Filament

Access Commodities - Accentuate

Sarah Bennett - Opalesence

Amy's Keeping Me In Stitches - Lacquered Jewels

DeDe Ogden - Prisms

This list is not exhaustive.

FRAMING TO BEST ADVANTAGE.

What is placed behind these canvases becomes a very important decision. Whatever is utilized, will be visible from the front and will become an integral part of the overall piece. Colored mat boards, or a fabric can be used. Take the stitched piece to the fabric store and play with various options until you find something that pleases you.

TABLE OF CONTENTS

STRAIGHT STITCHES

DIAGONAL STITCHES

CROSS STITCHES

PATTERN STITCHES

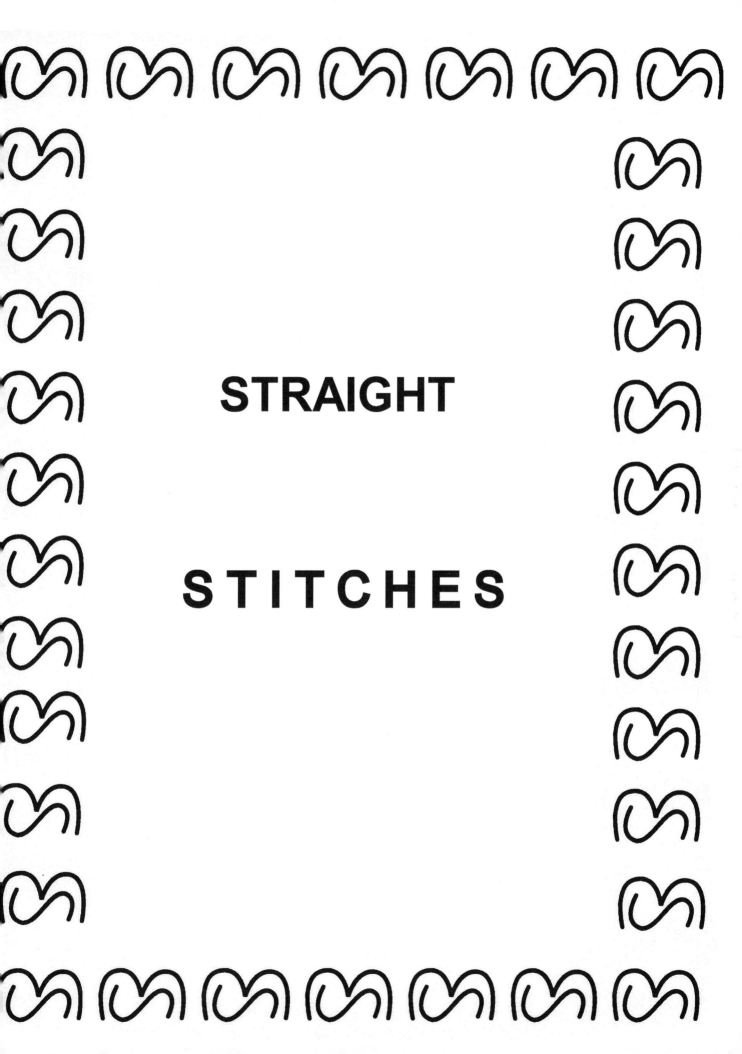

STRAIGHT

STITCHES

WOVEN PATTERN

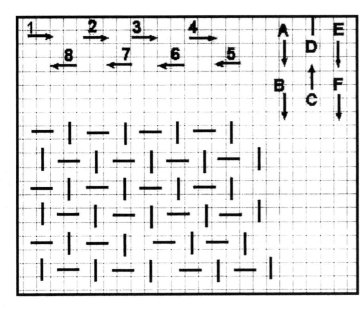

Model 1

Work all the Horizontal Stitches first and then fill in with the Vertical ones. Therefore, no thread will show from behind the canvas. The stitch has a woven appearance so is good for, but not limited to, items of clothing.

Sky, wallpaper, fabric, hats, socks

Compensation is not one of the favorite words of people who do needlepoint. The method of using lite stitches and fine threads allows the stitcher to forget that word. When you reach the edge of an area, and can no longer place a complete stitch in the space, stop. You do not have to compensate. There is enough blank canvas in the area,that the unstitched areas will not show.

The amazing thing is when the piece is finished, the eye believes it sees whole patterns even though it does not.

OPEN ZIG ZAG

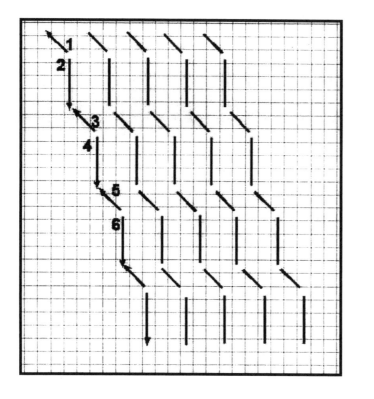

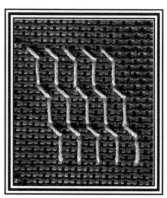

Model 1

Working back stitches in vertical rows keeps the thread from showing through. It can be done as numbered which is reversible. The spacing of the pattern can be varied to suit your needs. There could be a space between each stitch. The rows can be closer together or farther apart. The length of the individual stitches can also be altered, but remember to keep both long and short to get the zig zag effect.

Sky, fields, mountains

We often need to add strands when doing straight stitches to achieve full coverage. The reverse of this applies when we want lighter coverage. Straight stitches either horizontal or vertical are more apt to let the paint show through the canvas than diagonal stitches.

STRAIGHT MOSAIC VARIATIONS

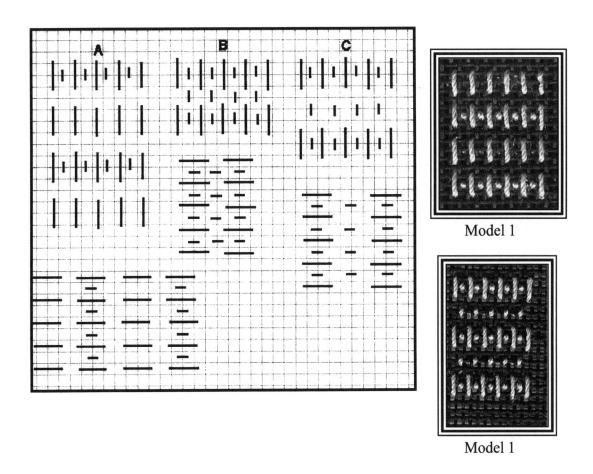

Model 1

Model 1

Three different versions of this pattern show how even a slight change in the arrangement of the individual stitches can make a substantial change in the overall appearance.

Clothing, bushes, tree tops,

I was taking a class from Deborah Wilson - Beau Geste. She said we should bring the canvas to our bodies, not stretching our bodies to reach the canvas. I thought it was a really great idea, and the whole time in class, I did exactly that.

When I got home, I was determined to continue this practice. Then I realized I had to work over the top of a very small dog who is firmly ensconced on my lap! The dog stays, I move my body!

OPEN GOBELIN

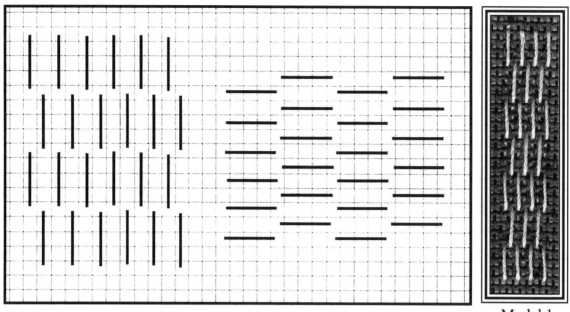

Model 1

Open Gobelin is an extremely versatile one that can be used in a variety of ways. The length of the Gobelins can be changed, even within the same canvas. An example of this is a background where you can make the stitches close to the main pattern over two canvas threads, while leaving those farther out over four threads.

Sky, trees, backgrounds

It is perfectly legal to photocopy your painted canvas - *for your use only.* This copy can serve several purposes. It can be helpful for the placement of trims or extra layers of stitching when the basic stitching is finished. A black and white copy can also help make the shading more obvious.

It can also be a good aid if you want to change colors on the canvas. The copy will help you get the gradations of the new color the same as those on the canvas.

STAIR STEP BACKSTITCHES

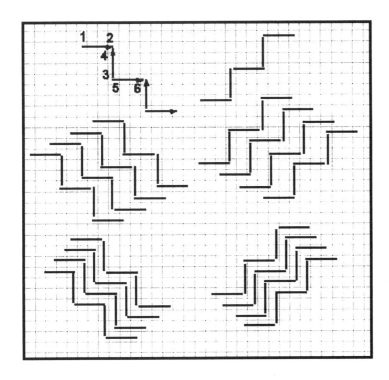

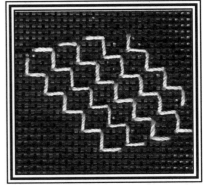

Model 1

Work in rows, doing a series of backstitches. There is a slight feeling of motion here, but it is not overwhelming.

Fields, bushes, trees, leaves, clothing

If the thread you are using tends to fray and ravel try using Fray Check™. To speed up the process, cut several lengths of thread and put a dab of Fray Check ™ on the end of each one as well as on the end of the thread still on the card or spool. When you have used the prepared pieces, you can cut off one more length which is already dry and ready to use. Repeat the process and use the length you just cut off the card first, allowing the others to dry.

Don't forget Fray check is also handy for stopping runs in hose. A word of caution, however, it goes through the hose and also sticks to your leg. Remove slowly and with care!

STAIR STEPS

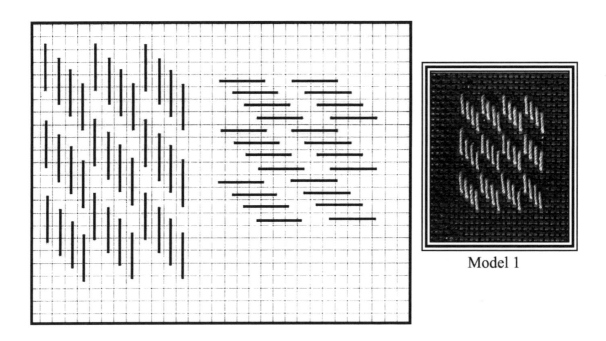

Model 1

The progression of this pattern seems to naturally work in diagonal rows. Stair Steps has a definite feeling of movement.

If used for clothing, the direction of the movement can be altered to indicate the division between sleeves and body of a garment.

Water, mountains, fields, clothing

Sometimes there is a decorative area on a canvas that needs to be added after the rest of the piece is stitched. One idea for adding the area to a canvas is to transfer the area onto tracing paper - the thinner the tracing paper, the better. Stitch the rest of the area in the basic stitch you are using, going right over the paint. Then pin the tracing paper down onto the canvas, and carefully stitch through the paper onto the top of the previous stitching. A sharp needle can be very helpful for this part.

After finishing stitching, carefully tear off or cut away the tracing paper. A pair of tweezers can be extremely helpful at this point to remove the small bits of paper.

OPEN STRAIGHT ORIENTAL

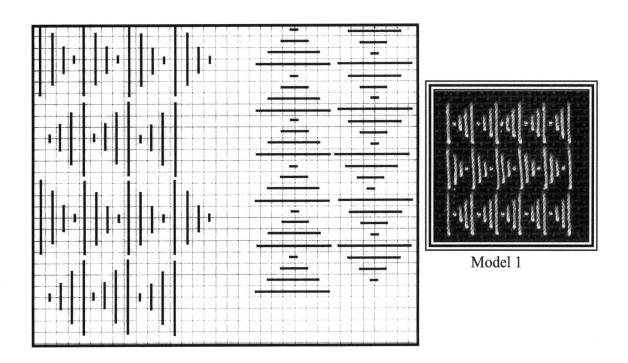

Model 1

Work in horizontal rows. Since this Oriental is a fairly large stitch, it moves quickly and is a good choice for large backgrounds which can handle some texture. It can fit around a main pattern fairly well. By doing just part of the stitch to fit into areas, the eye assumes the entire pattern is there.

Mountains, fields, water, wall paper, curtains, umbrellas

Leaving a needlework market, I shared a taxi with a woman who works for a knitting company. After sharing introductions, she told me she always buys at least one painted canvas during the Market. No, she does not do needlepoint, but after looking at them all week end, she has to own another one. She plans on buying ocean front property, sitting in a rocking chair and stitching when she retires.

I told her I would gladly join her, and teach her to stitch!

MILANESE VARIATION

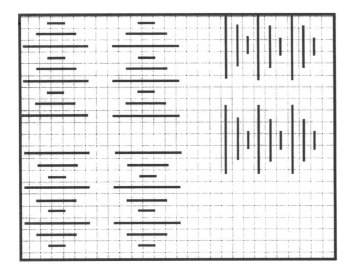

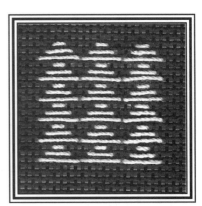

Model 1

Milanese Variation is also worked in rows to prevent the thread from showing through. There is less pattern than is created by the Oriental Stitch. It also works well for larger backgrounds.

Fields, mountains, clothing, sky, curtains

There are times when it is necessary to place a needle under thread that is already in place. (When you are doing a pin tuck, or a locking L to finish a thread.) Here is a situation that is a good place to use your laying tool. Place it very gently between the threads to be separated or under the threads to be lifted, and slide your needle down. A wooden laying tool is good for this practice, since it is less apt to split the threads already in place.

MINI DIAMONDS

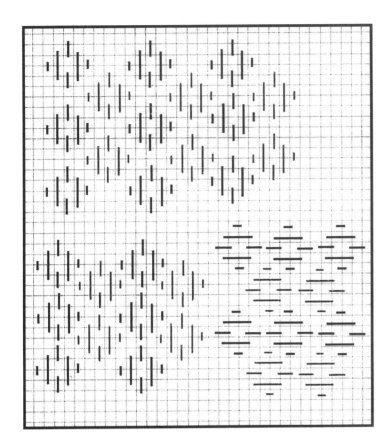

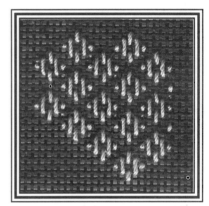

Model 1

The graph is shown in two colors to make it easier to distinguish the rows. The stitch could be done in two colors/threads if desired, but is equally effective with just one. There is quite a lot of texture to the stitch.

Clothing, flowers, shrubbery, hats, sky, snow

Be careful what you have on your lap when you are stitching. Other objects may find their way onto the back of your canvas without your being aware of their attachment.

If the object is your nightgown, you may decide to cut the material rather than ripping the stitching. However, if it is a good dress, you will probably have to remove the stitching.

From personal experience, if it is a little white dog, either remove stitching carefully or give the dog a lopsided hair cut.

GOBELIN BY THREE

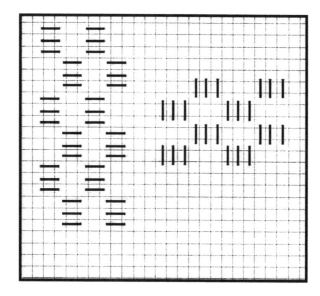

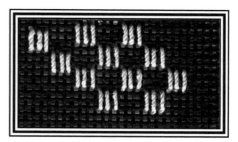

Model 1

This simple little group of straight stitches gives you several choices.

The method of stitching could either be a darning pattern or working them in groups of three moving diagonally down the canvas. It could be done as a couching pattern with a different thread underneath. When there is a couched thread underneath, stitching in rows across would cover the travel threads.

Bushes, flowers, clothing, grass

Sometimes there are large and small sections on the same area - like a snowman body and head, which you want to look somewhat alike, but not identical. Consider doing two stitches that are similar such as Scotch and Mosaic. You can also do the same stitch in both areas but change the size of the stitch used. Cashmere and variations shown in the Introduction or Open Diagonal on page 4 are examples.

OPEN TWILL

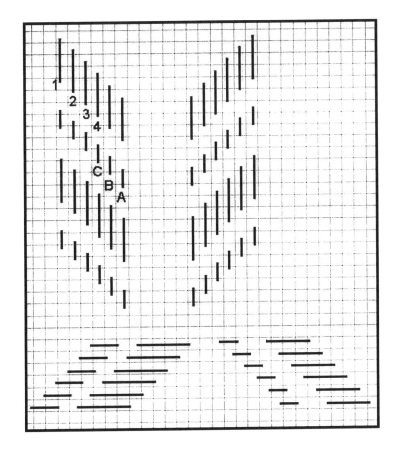

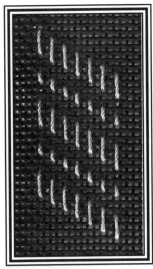

OPEN TWILL

Open twill is a good choice for using two colors/threads. The length of the stitch can be altered, and the number of threads between rows can also be changed.

Work in rows, stepping by one thread.

Water, hillsides, beaches, clothing, bushes

If you are doing a long border of Cross Stitches or Smyrnas, do just one leg of the stitch for the entire border. Count once again to make sure you have the correct number of stitches, then come back and complete the stitch on a second pass. It is easier and faster to just count the one leg.

If you count incorrectly, there is less to rip using this system!

PILLARS

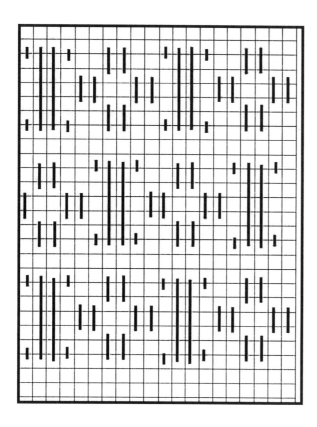

Model 1

Pillars also gives you an option for using two colors/threads. If you are using one color/thread, work in horizontal rows. If two colors, try working diagonally.

The stitch creates a definite pattern, so it should go where a design will enhance the overall canvas.

Walls, buildings, Santa's bag, Santa's sleigh

A photocopy of your work after you have completed a project is also useful. The copy can help you remember threads and stitches used in the piece. It is especially nice for the projects you give away. With a copy, you can always have a reminder of what you did.

Be sure to note on the copy the threads and stitches you used to work the piece. A separate stitch guide, or writing on the back will keep you from forgetting.

ROLLING ARROWS

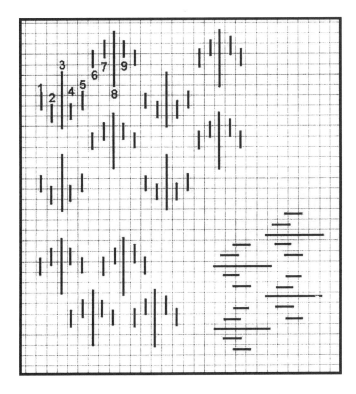

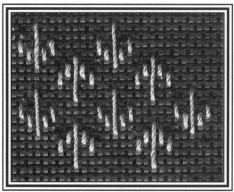

Model 1

Although the numbering shows working horizontally, it can also be done diagonally. Rolling arrows is a little stitch that has quite a bit of design. By going in the same direction, it can be used for trees, or umbrellas.

Trees, bushes, clothing, hillsides, umbrellas

Dana and her husband were having dinner at a Chinese restaurant. Suddenly Dana got all excited and was making strange noises. Her husband was concerned there might be a fly in her soup.

"Oh no," she replied, "my place mat will make a great pattern for the sampler I am stitching!"

Of course, then she had to keep her place mat clean or explain why she wanted a new one to take home.

BENJAMIN

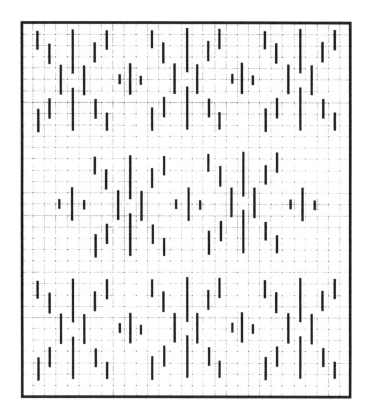

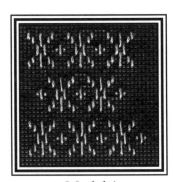

Model 1

Since some of the thread will show through from the back as you move through this stitch, the stitching thread should be close to the canvas thread in color. You can also execute Benjamin as a darning pattern, where you expect the thread to show through, the thread can be any color.

Borders, clothing, wallpaper, sky

Barbara commented that Mary's 'Toodle oos' were not very big. Everyone asked what in the world 'toodle-oos' were, since the only obvious thing was they were part of the body.

Barbara responded, "Remember when you were leaving and your Grandmother would wave good-bye, saying 'Toodle-Oo!'? Her upper arms would be waving as she said this so those are your 'toodle-oos!'

LANTERNS

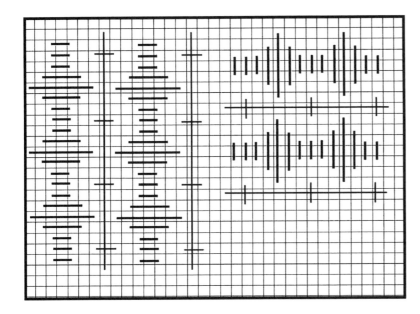

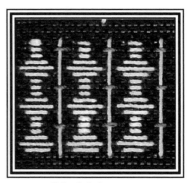

Model 1

The design, created by Lanterns, gives you a choice of using one, two or even three colors/threads. The first example should be worked in vertical rows and the second one in horizontal rows.

Wallpaper, curtains, borders

You can make the same color bead look different by changing the color of the thread you use to attach the bead. Try making a sampler of beads with different threads and see the effects you can achieve. Obviously the lighter the bead, the bigger the difference.

COUCHING PATTERN A

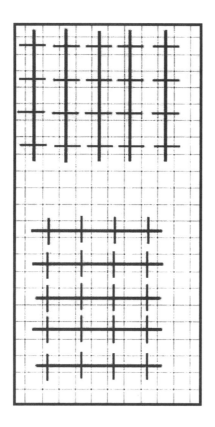

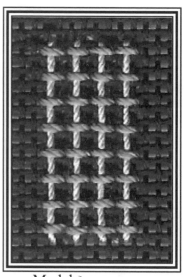

Model 1

This simple pattern fits into small spaces. The choice of threads can make a more dramatic statement. If you are looking for subtle way to fill an area, this could be a good choice. The less contrast the threads have, the more subtle it is. Couching patterns work up fairly quickly.

Clothing, beaches, packages, angel's wings, baskets

Raising children taught me that the words "never and always" should never be applied to children. As soon as I said "My child never..." or "My child always..." they proved me wrong.

It is my belief that it also applies to needlework. As soon as we say we should never or always do something a certain way, some new technique comes along and the old hard and fast rule no longer applies!

COUCHING PATTERN B

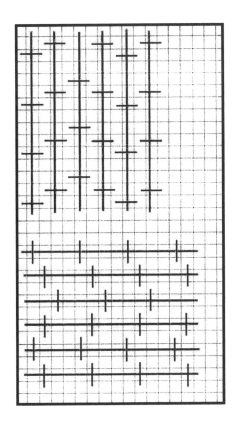

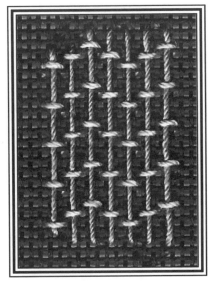

Model 1

This pattern creates a subtle feeling of movement.

Water, beaches, clouds, hillsides, umbrellas

My mother taught my sister and me to do needlepoint. We "always" used tapestry wool and "never" did anything except the Continental Stitch.

In our later lives, my sister owned a needlepoint shop, where she sold hundreds of fibers. I have written stitch books with several hundred stitches.

A case in point - "always" no longer applies.

COUCHING PATTERN C

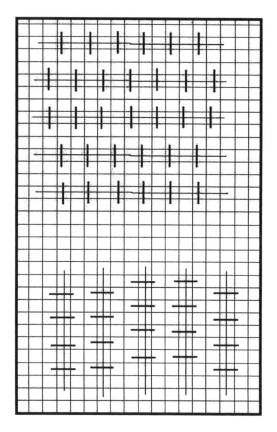

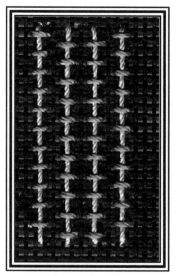

Model 1

By changing the spacing of the rows slightly, a different effect emerges. There is no motion or movement with this choice.

Clothing, clouds, beaches, grass, baskets

To cause an area of stitching to "pop up," work a row of outline stitches around it. The eye will hardly notice the stitches, unless they are in a contrasting color, but the area will be more dominant.

COUCHING PATTERN D

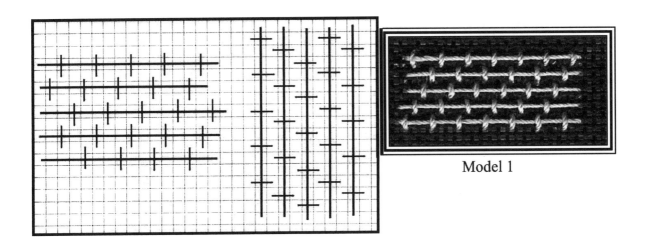

Model 1

Here is a pattern that flows to the left, although if worked upside down, it would flow to the right. Again by changing the rows of the original stitch only slightly, the whole effect of the stitch changes. You might want to try using some graph paper and "experimenting" with different placements.

Snow, water, clouds, umbrellas, packages

If you are framing a geometric piece, place four hangers on the back. Then you can turn the piece to have a different perspective, depending on your mood. You can also make scheduled changes - every month or when the seasons change.

This system can cause your spouse to think you have new pictures more often. "Honey, see how many things I have finished!"

ARISTEIA COUCHING

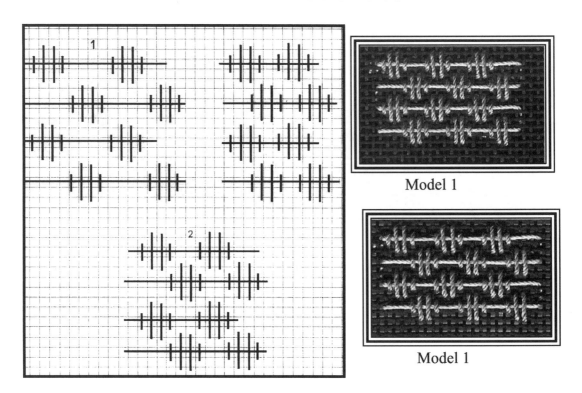

Model 1

Model 1

Wendy Harwood from Aristeia Needlepoint Shop in Los Angeles showed me this stitch. It is an excellent example of taking a popular stitch (Hungarian) and changing it slightly to create a different look. Consider using other well known stitches for couching patterns. Keep this idea in mind when you look at stitch books.

Clothing, wallpaper, borders, packages

Needles, as well as scissors, can be affected by metallic threads. In a perfect stitching area, there should be separate needles for metallic threads. If you are not quite that organized, you may be using the same needles for everything.

If you suddenly find your silk threads (or any other) fraying, you may need to use a new needle which has never been used for metallic threads.

RAILWAY TRACKS

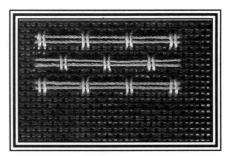

Model 1

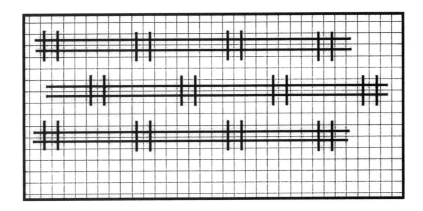

This stitch got its name because I used it underneath a train, thinking it looked like tracks. Railway Tracks requires a fairly large space to be effective. If a large space is not available, then the distance between the straight stitches could be changed to suit the area.

Railway tracks, borders, walls

If you are having trouble doing a stitch, especially one you have done before, leave it alone. Do something else for awhile, stitch something else, or worse yet do some housework. When you get back to the stitch, it will go much easier.

RAILROAD BACKGROUND

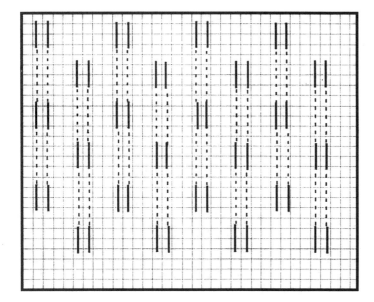
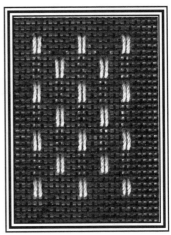

Model 1

Here is the darning pattern I used on the piece with the Railway Tracks. It is a quick stitch that can be very subtle. Using a thread that matches the canvas color will give the appearance of the entire background being stitched.

If a more striking look is desired, consider a metallic thread in either a matching or a contrasting color.

Clothing, grass, sky, water

Lorelee was knitting a pair of socks. She was using four needles and suddenly realized she had a different design on each of the needles. One of the designs was correct and the other three were "mistakes."

We told her that we thought anyone could follow a pattern, but it takes real creativity to end up with four designs from just one pattern!.

HUNGARIAN BARGELLO A

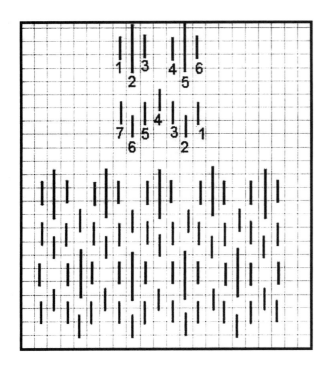

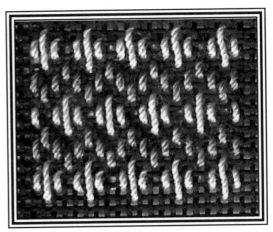

Model 1

Here is another example of taking a popular stitch, changing it slightly and adding space for an open look. The Bargello could be omitted, leaving the more open Hungarian.

Working in Horizontal rows allows you the option of using two colors/threads, although one is also very effective.

Water, sky, mountains, clothing, Santa's sleigh, packages

Threads are like children. If they are out of sight, they are apt to be causing problems and getting into trouble. Therefore, if you are using two or more needles, bring the needle not in use to the front of your canvas.

Do not be tempted to say, "I only have one stitch, I'm sure I can control it that long." You can't! (Yes, I know because I have tried and gotten major messes on the back of the canvas!)

HUNGARIAN BARGELLO B

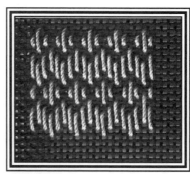

Model 1

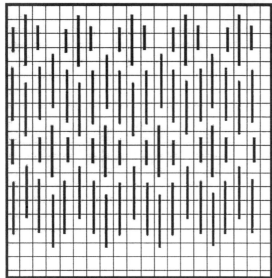 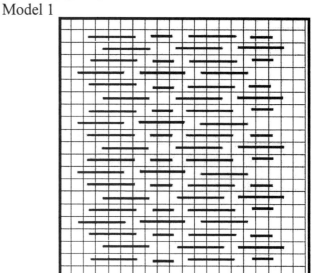

A slightly larger version of Hungarian Bargello A, which could be worked in either horizontal or vertical rows. The diamond patterns will be more noticeable if you use a thread that matches the canvas for the Bargello and a contrast for the Hungarian.

Mountains, clouds, sky, clothing, hillsides, water

Some threads are too fragile to use to stitch with, because they will fray from going in and out of the canvas holes. However, that does not mean we can't find other ways to use them. They can be couched onto a canvas with a stronger thread. They could also be used as wraps, as in a Spider Web or a Wrapped Chain.

VERTICAL WAVE

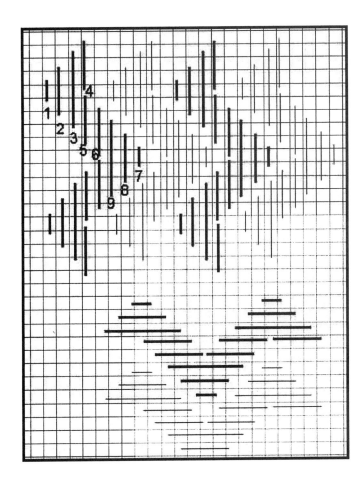

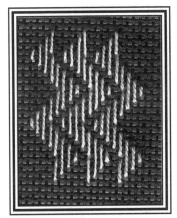

Model 1

The progression of the stitch seems to be easiest following the rows, completing each "wave" before beginning the next wave. The lighter lines are shown on the graph to help delineate the rows, although they can be a second color/thread.

Smoke, water, sky, mountains, walls

If you think you can find a use for a unique thread, bead or other form of embellishment, you probably will. It is better to buy it when you see it to add to your collection.

Otherwise, someday, when you have the perfect place for it, it is in someone else's collection gathering dust rather than in your stitching room when you need it!.

DIAGONAL HUNGARIAN

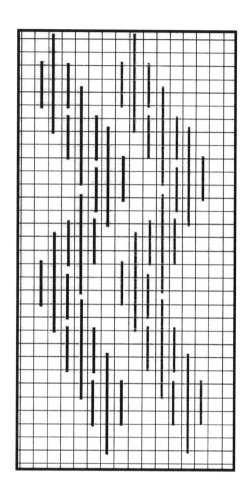

Model 1

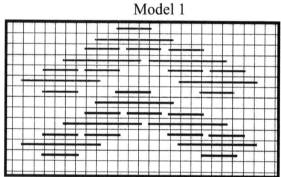

The working order for this stitch would be the same as for the Vertical Wave. It is a Hungarian stitch that works up in a diagonal flow. More than one color/thread could be used effectively.

There is a repeat of three Hungarian patterns going in one direction, and then three going in the other direction. The number of repeats could be changed to make the pattern larger or smaller.

Water, streams, hills, wallpaper, smoke

If you are having trouble with a thread getting knotted and tangled, try making the tail shorter.

HORIZONTAL WAVES

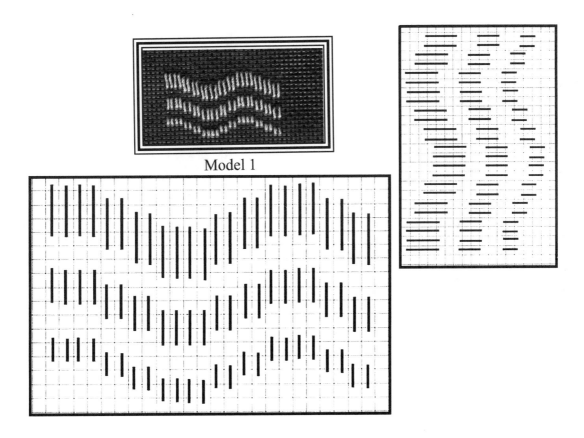

Model 1

There are many options for this pattern since the number of Gobelin stitches in each repeat could be changed. It requires quite a large area as it is graphed, but could easily be done with more repeats by decreasing the number of stitches in each repeat.

The rows could be reversed, placing the smaller rows on the top rather than the bottom.

Water, sky, clouds, grass, smoke

One way to chart a border around your design is to use a long piece of thread. Baste it with long running stitches where you think you will want the border. If it is not right, you can easily remove the thread and reposition it. Then if you want to mark the canvas you can, or you can just leave the thread in place as a marking.

OPEN VICTORIAN STEP

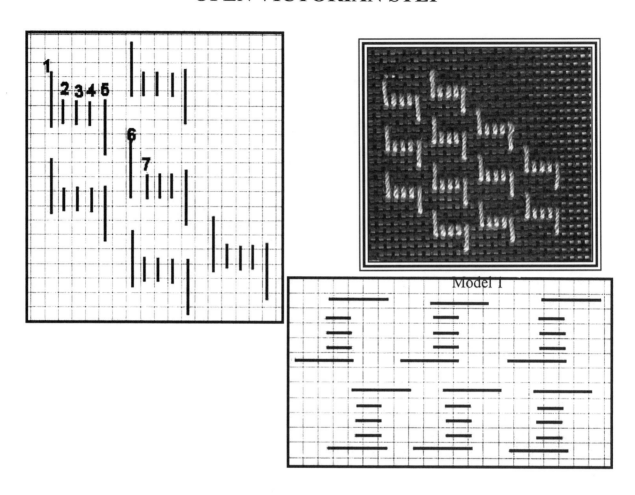

Model 1

Victorian Step can be opened up - spread out so there are spaces between the stitches. It seems easiest to work the stitch diagonally, although it can also be done in horizontal rows. If you wanted to add a second color/thread, use for alternating diagonal rows.

Clothing, walls, Santa's bag, Santa's sleigh, snow

There is much discussion about the importance of the backs of needlework pieces. My friend Penny says, "The back is only important as it affects the front of the work!" That seems to me to be a good definition.

If you are doing something questionable, check to see if it affects the front.

ELK MOUNTAIN

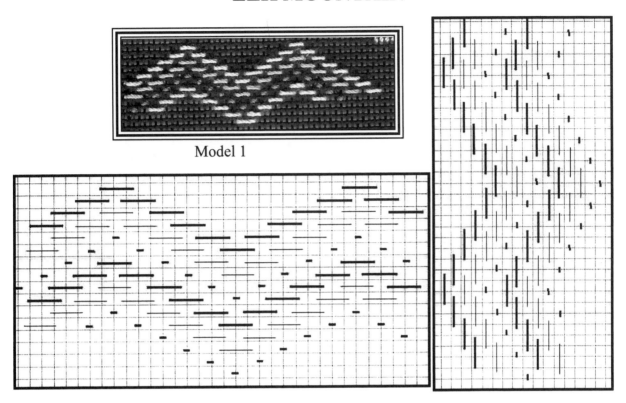

Model 1

Here is a choice which allows a lot of paint to show through.

This stitch can be confusing, however, and needs to be counted very carefully. The three different lines on the graph were done that way to help delineate the rows. They do not necessarily denote three colors/threads, although they could.

Water, mountains, streams, hills, smoke

We have been taught for years not to put knots on the back of our work. Now we embellish canvases with beads, baubles and bangles of all sorts. If the knot on the back is smaller than the things on the front, we may go ahead and use it. Check the front, however, to make sure the knot is not creating a bump.

TRIPLETS

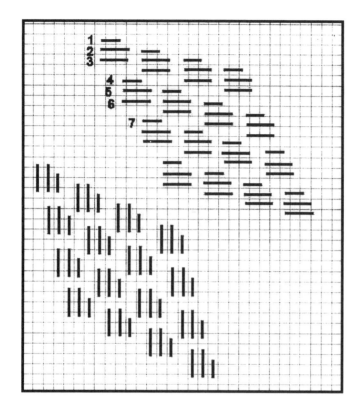

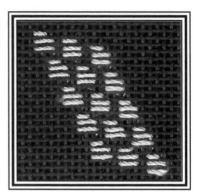

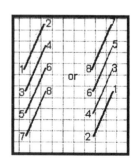

Model 1

Triplets, named because it consists of groups of three stitches, will not give much pattern. It is subtle, and if the thread and canvas are close in color, the canvas will barely show. It could be worked horizontally as well as diagonally.

Clothing, bushes, flowers, shrubbery, snow

The usual suggestion is to form a stitch the direction you are traveling. If you are going from the bottom to the top of a row, enter the canvas from the top of the stitch and then complete by going into the canvas at the bottom of the stitch. This path gives the maximum coverage to your stitches.

WAVES

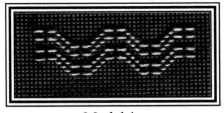

Model 1

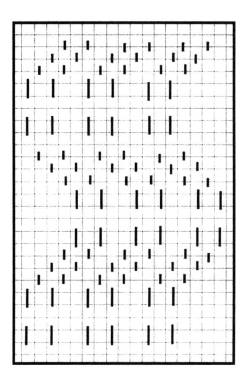

If you have a canvas where you want just a little thread and a great deal of paint showing, here is a very good choice. Work as a series of back stitches going across the rows and then back again. A fine metallic thread would add glitter and a slight bit of pattern.

Water, mountains, fields, floors, walls, trees, smoke

Sometimes silver beads have a tendency to turn black after they have been exposed to the air for awhile.

If you spray them with Aqua Net™ Hair Spray, the problem can be prevented. Spray them and let them dry completely before stitching them onto your canvas. (I was told the reason for the Aqua Net brand is because it is the cheapest, other brands will probably work.)

You can also use Krylon™. Place the beads in a plastic bag and spray the Krylon into the bag. Shake well, after closing the bag, to coat all the beads evenly and prevent their sticking together.

DIAGONAL

STITCHES

OPEN DIAGONAL WEAVE

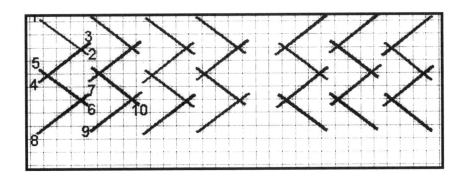

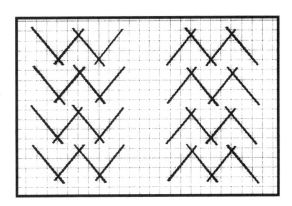

Model 2

Work this stitch in rows, as in the graph, to avoid thread showing through from the back. It is graphed over four canvas threads, but the size could be altered as desired for a particular area.

Clothing, sky, clouds

Before you buy a canvas, there are some questions you should ask yourself. (If you are not planning to stitch the piece, and just add it to your collection, then you can skip this page.)

Is it stitchable? Is it a good design? Do I want to stitch the design? If your answers are yes, then go ahead with the purchase.

If the answers are "no," but you really love the piece, then go ahead and buy it. You know there are many other projects in line ahead of this one.

PLAITED STITCH

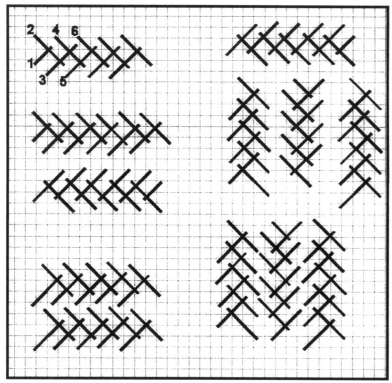

Model 2

Plaited Stitch, when worked with space between the rows, gives the appearance of a tight stitch, while still allowing the paint to show through.

When the rows alternate, the design appears less striped.

Wallpaper, stripes, floors, clothing, packages, bushes, tree leaves

If you do not love a canvas, life is too short to stitch it. If you ever find yourself willingly doing housework before stitching a particular canvas, you should not be doing that project.

Put it away - there are lots of others waiting for you! Better yet, give it to someone who will love it!

TRELLIS STITCH

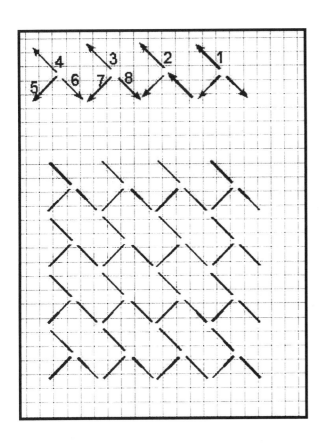

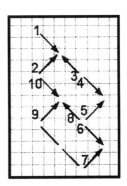

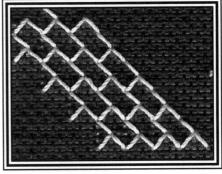

Model 2

Trellis Stitch is one that works up fairly quickly. There are two ways shown to do the stitch. Either one is perfectly acceptable; it is a matter of preference. The second way shows less thread from the back, but takes more thought and planning ahead.

Fences, walls, floors

Needlework is a hobby. It is however not a hobby that is always dependent on progress. It is a collection hobby. Other examples of collection hobbies are stamps, coins, paintings and rare books.

DIAGONAL GOBELIN

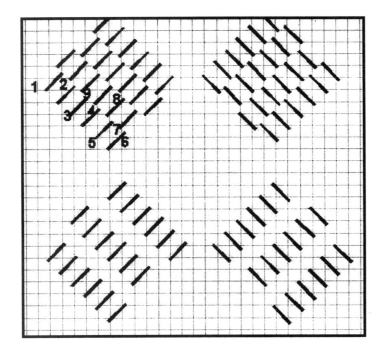

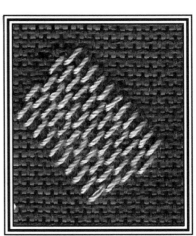

Model 2

Here is a choice that could go almost anywhere. It has minimal pattern, and does let most of the paint show through.

Clothing, snow, flowers, leaves, packages

If you have one of something, it is stuff.
If you have two of something, it is a collection.
If you have a collection, you must collect more!
Collecting obviously includes canvases, threads, accessories, stands, and books.

MOSAIC VARIATION A

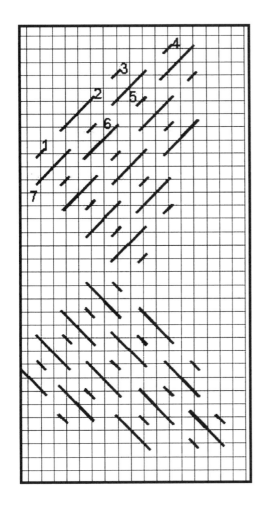

Model 2

By stitching the variation as a series of back stitches (as counted in the graph), the thread showing through from the back is kept to a minimum.

If the stitch is done in diagonal rows the thread from the back would make an interesting pattern. In other words, work from 1 to 7 and on down the row diagonally.

It is a quick stitch pattern that fits almost anywhere. With a fine thread, the paint shows through nicely.

Clothing, bushes, fabric, flowers, sky, clouds, snow

"Needlepoint is a therapeutic addiction that is legal." - - Don Upde of Lee's Needleworks.

MOSAIC VARIATION B

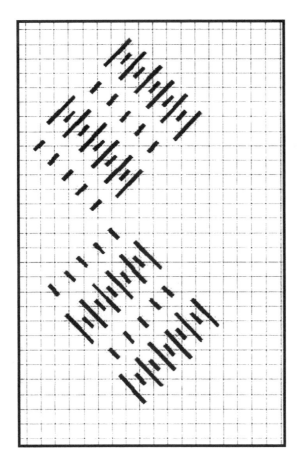

Model 2

Mosaic Variation B is a slight variation from the previous page which is somewhat tighter, though still quite open.

Clothing, snow, clouds, sky

"Art washes away from the soul the dust of everyday life." - - Pablo Picasso
I love the saying for two reasons. First it encourages my creativity. However, even more important, if my husband mentions dust, I can tell him that with all the needlework around the house, the soul can't be bothered by the dust.

MOSAIC VARIATION C

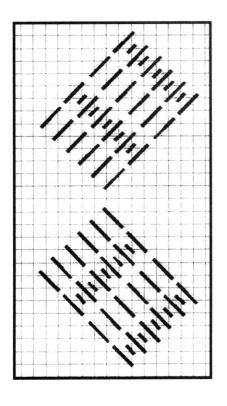

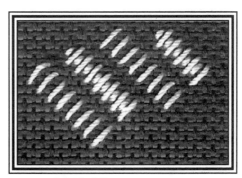

Model 2

These three Mosaic variations (see previous two pages) demonstrate how changing just a small portion of the way the stitch is counted changes the pattern. Here is a choice that is good to stitch two parts of the same thing - a snowman's head and his body. By using two different variations of the same stitch, the pattern is changed, but not drastically. The result becomes easier on the eye.

Here is a versatile stitch that can go almost anywhere.

Clothing, sky, snow, snowman

Shortly after Kitty bought a needlepoint shop, her mother died. There were several things which had belonged to her mother that went to an auction, as neither Kitty nor her sister wanted them. One of these was a small sewing stand that had been painted pink during the 1950's. This rickety object can only be described as "ugly!"

The day of the sale, Kitty had to work, so her husband Bill and a friend went to the sale in her place. Bill was so extremely proud of his purchase. He said it would be just perfect in the new shop. He still can not understand why Kitty was not also thrilled with the pink wicker sewing stand that he bought and carefully brought home!

OPEN SERENDIPITY

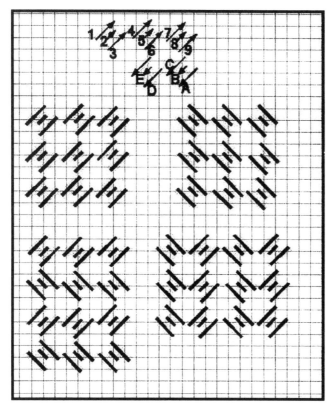

Model 2

Notice that the graph shows the patterns going both in the same direction and also in opposite directions. The direction of the individual patterns can vary the appearance quite a lot.

There is room in either choice to place another pattern if you don't want so much open area in your design.

Wallpaper, floors, clouds, snow

Another name for stash is Personal Resource Center. That has the sound of something very important - which it is!

OPEN DIAGONAL SCOTCH

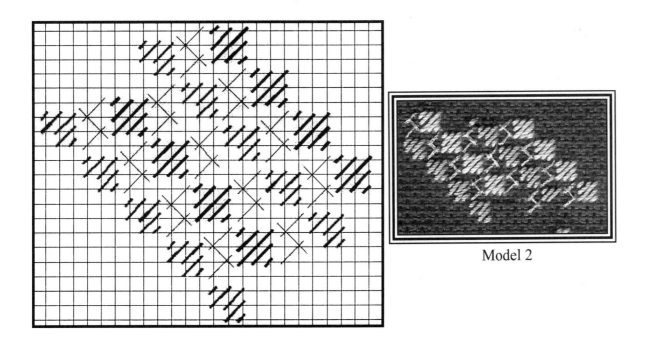

Model 2

This Scotch Variation has a lot of pattern. The basic Scotch Stitch is stitched with Elegance and the smaller stitches are done with a metallic .

I find it easier to work the Scotch stitches first and then fill in with the diagonals. These can be done with a finer thread, although that is not necessary. The Scotch stitches are shown with two different lines showing that they can be two colors/threads. They can also be very effective with one color.

Clothing, wallpaper, packages, snow, snowmen

The stitch guides that come with some painted canvases often reflect the preferences of the person who wrote them. That does not mean they will always reflect your preferences. If the thread and/or stitch is something you do not like - change it!

They are called Stitch Guides, not Stitch Commandments!

OPEN ORIENTAL

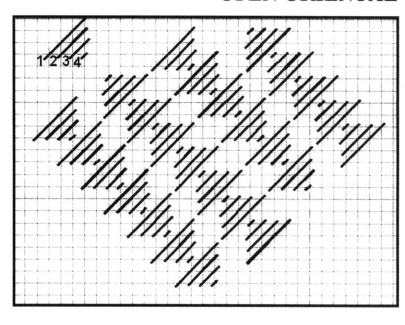

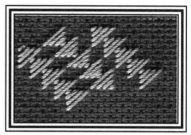

Model 2

Open Oriental is best done in diagonal rows. Two colors of thread could be used if that is preferable. Two different threads of the same color can also be very effective.

There is a definite diagonal flow to the stitch.

Hillsides, snow, clouds

Working with silk, especially flat silk, can be a challenge.

One suggestion is to keep the silk off the surface of the canvas. Use a laying tool to keep it away from the canvas.

Silk can snag on the rough spots on hands, even the ones we don't know are there. Therefore it is best to handle the silk as little as possible and keep your hands as smooth as possible. An emery board rubbed over the rough spots helps .

Hold the silk perpendicular to the canvas when you take it to the back.

NICOLE A

Model 2

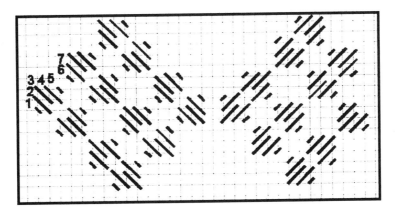

I found this pattern without a name, so decided to name it for my newest granddaughter.

It can be done in one or two colors/threads. If you chose to use two, they can be alternated by rows going in either direction.

It also has a diagonal flow to its appearance which limits its uses.

Snow, mountains, shrubbery

There are many solutions for the rough hand problem many of us have. One is a good hand cream applied often, but <u>not</u> right before stitching. The best thing I have found (and I have tried a lot) is the Mary Kay hand treatment.

If you have areas of roughness on your hands, you can cover these with Super Glue. The glue not only keeps the thread from snagging, it protects your hands so they can heal.

NICOLE B

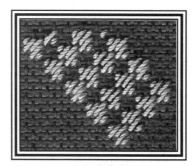

Model 2

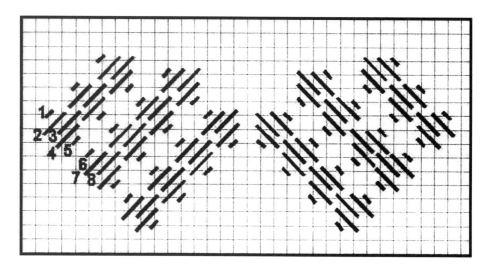

Notice that there is a set of five stitches that are grouped together to form the pattern. The sets above are arranged differently to form the three Nicole stitches. Other arrangements of the five stitches are also good alternatives.

Snow, clouds, sky, hillsides

Ruth and Rita were at a stitching retreat. There was a commotion in the room. Rita looked up to see Ruth laying on the floor. She was surrounded by several people. Ruth complained that her best friend did not even come to her aid.

Rita explained, "I was stitching and I had a deadline for the piece I was doing. I do have my priorities!"

I do not think Ruth was pleased with her response.

NICOLE C

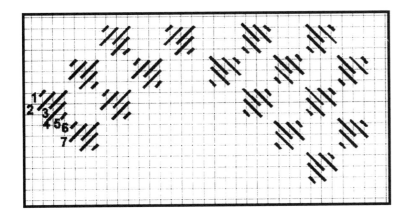

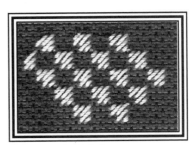

Model 2

Nicole C is the most open of the three Nicole stitches. It may be filled in with a Scotch Stitch going in the opposite direction with a second color/thread.

Working in diagonal rows seems to be the best way to keep the open spaces clean.

Clothing, snow, mountains, flowers

I was working at our local shop and a customer told me she needed to buy some beading projects. She said she does these bead projects at night when she can't sleep. I have several friends who are convinced that beading causes insomnia, but surely does not cure it. I guess we are not all alike!

DROPPED MOSAIC

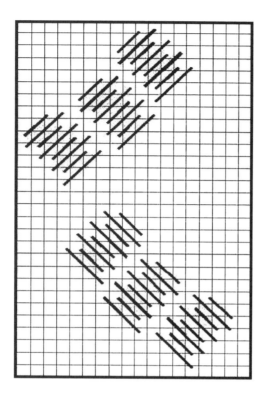

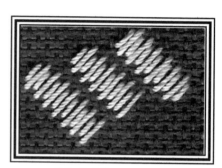

Model 2

The stitched areas are fairly dense so the openness of the pattern comes from the distance between stitches. The spacing can be altered to be farther apart, therefore more open. A thin thread could be used to place a tent stitch in the blank area.

Clothing, clouds, snow, Santa's sleigh

Remember to place your piece away from you once in awhile when you are stitching. We all work with our canvases right up to our faces, but then hang them and everyone looks at them from a distance. Since this is the way they will be ultimately viewed, we should view them this way while they are a work in "progress."

It is also a good idea to hang a finished piece where it you can view it at different times during the day. You can decide if there are any areas that bother you that need to be changed before it is framed!

LARGE WOVEN STITCH

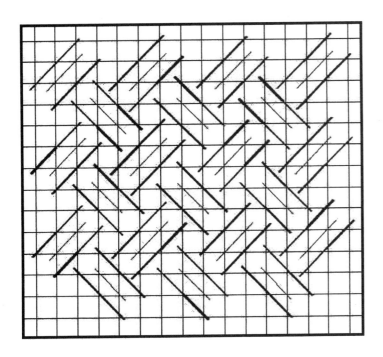

Model 2

The model was stitched with Elegance for the thicker line and Subtlety for the thinner line. The line could be left unstitched or a very fine thread can be used. There is no diagonal feel to this pattern.

Clothing, Santa's sleigh, baskets, pillows, fabric

When you look at a canvas to begin planning what to stitch, decide where you want the focal point to be. This area is often, but not always, the largest object or the one in front. The focal point is where you want to draw the most attention. Once identified, you can plan the other areas. The focal point is not necessarily where you want to begin stitching.

DIAGONAL STITCHES

CROSS

STITCHES

CRAZY CROSSES A

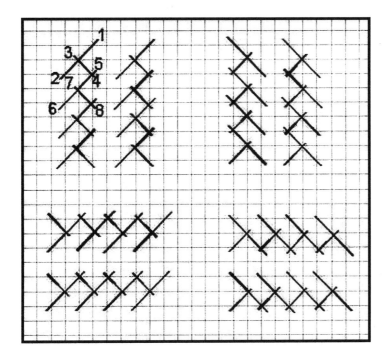

Model 2

Crazy Crosses A needs to be worked from top to bottom. Cut the thread and work from the top down again. It is a 'tight open' stitch that can fit in small areas.

It could be used as the divider between two patterns for a background.

Stripes, cuffs, collars, braid

It usually seems like a good idea to begin stitching a canvas with an area you know exactly how to stitch. A good example of such an area would be a face. You are probably going to do Basketweave with floss or silk. While you are working on this area, you have a chance to study other places on the canvas and begin to make decisions.

CRAZY CROSSES B

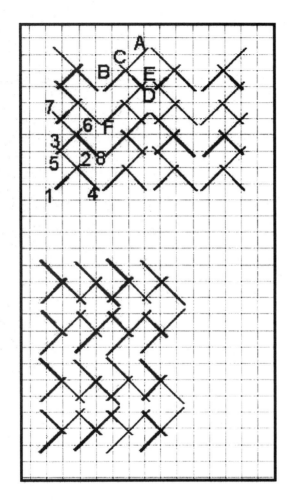

Model 2

Crazy Crosses B reverses the direction of every row. This reversal creates a wider pattern area. Work the stitch from top to bottom and then back from bottom to top.

Stripes, cuffs, borders, clothing

Metallic canvas is now available with gold, silver or opalescent threads running though it. These metallic threads occur only on the weft, not the warp of the canvas. If you use a vertical stitch, you will cover most of the canvas. Therefore, it is better to chose horizontal stitches with the metallic canvases.

OBLONG CROSS VARIATION A

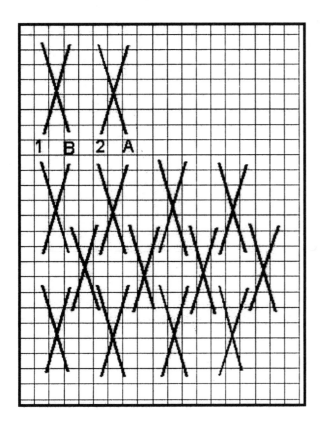

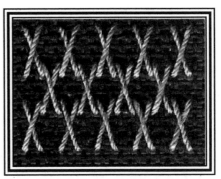

Model 2

It seems best to work Oblong Cross Variation in two passes. The second row will cover the thread that would show through from the back.

Bushes, shrubbery, mountains

I had spilled part of a soft drink onto about a dozen Floss Away Bags.™ Of course the bags became quite sticky, so I decide to wash them. I carefully washed them inside and out and placed them onto paper towels on the kitchen counter.

I had to repeat the process the next two days. When my husband came home from work, he studied the bags on the counter. He asked, "What are you doing?"

I explained the problem and said so far I had been unable to get rid of the sticky substance.

He just smiled and asked quietly, "Just how much do those bags cost apiece?"

I realized that the amount of my cost saving was not worth the effort I was expending. I threw away the bags!

OBLONG CROSS VARIATION B

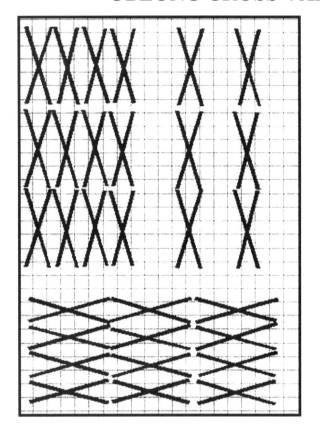

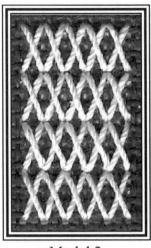

Model 2

This version of Oblong Cross creates a tighter pattern. If done in rows, there is a straight stitch showing through. If done consistently throughout, it becomes a form of darning pattern.

If you prefer a more open look, leave more spaces between the rows, as shown in the upper right section of the graph. The number of open spaces can vary.

Clothing, trees, bushes, flowers, walls

Stitching bags are another collectable item for needleworkers. Having several of them in what I believe is every imaginable size, why do I never have the size I need when and where I need it? I believe this qualifies as another addition to Murphy's law.

GOBELIN CROSS A

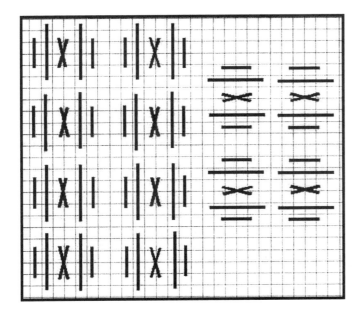

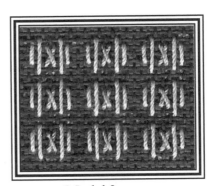

Model 2

Combining two stitches, Gobelin and Oblong Cross, can create something entirely different. It is a pattern with almost unlimited uses. The spaces between the units can be altered to fit whatever area is being worked. Cross stitches could also be placed between every row, appearing less like stripes.

The model is stitched with two colors but it can also be very effective with just one color.

Clothing, walls, flowers, wallpaper, flooring, borders

Stitching bags and purses have one thing in common. They are always too big and too full. I do not understand why the item we need most and use most often is always at the bottom of these bags. If we are always using it, how can it get to the bottom so quickly?

GOBELIN CROSS B

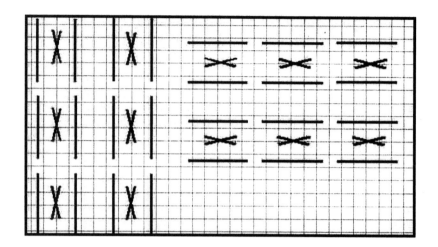

The shorter Gobelin stitch has been dropped to create a different unit. This choice can be used in many places and stitches up quite quickly. By working in vertical rows, the change in color is easily accomplished. The second color/thread is not really necessary since one color also looks good.

Clothing, bushes, clouds, walls, floors, borders

If there were no problems, we would not need to find solutions. Solutions are the beginning of creativity. We should learn to love problems. I must admit, I have not reached this point.

Problems can also be called opportunities. I know a group of men who meet every week to talk over their "opportunities" and discuss possible solutions.

CROSS VARIATION A

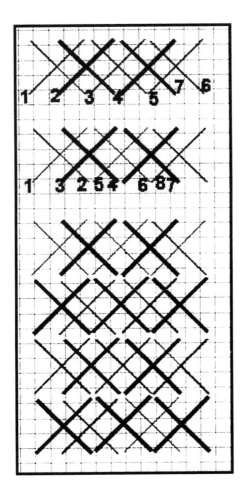

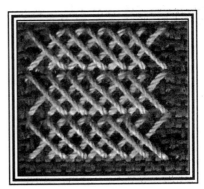

Model 2

The graph is done with two different line styles to delineate between the two crosses. However, one color is probably preferable. If you want to try two, I suggest practicing on a doodle canvas to see how it will look.

This variation is done by working each row in two passes (top graph) or all at the same time as shown in the second graph.

Clothing, stripes, bushes, trees (worked in vertical rows)

To visualize how a stitch looks if done in a different direction, turn the book that way. However, do not turn both the canvas and the book, or you will be going in the original direction. Squinting helps you see the final effect.

CROSS VARIATION B

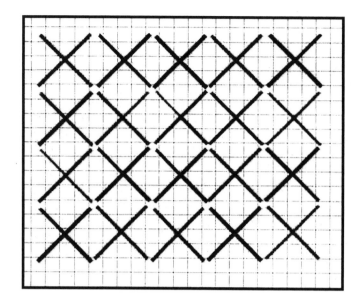

Model 2

This Cross variation can be worked in rows as suggested with the previous stitch. A vertical line will show through the canvas as can be seen in the model. The line can be covered with an upright stitch after the crosses were completed.

Borders, bushes, walls, wallpaper, floors

Color is more intense in large quantities. Therefore, when selecting color, try and look at just a single strand. You may want to go one shade lighter than you think you will need.

Beads are also much more intense in the packages than they are when you are applying one at a time to a canvas.

ENTWINED CROSS

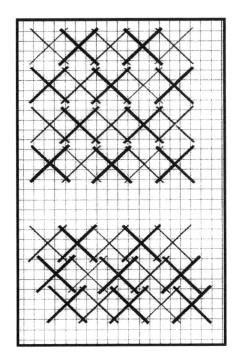

Model 2

I find the different arrangements of cross stitches fascinating. This cross variation and the previous two all start with the exact same basic stitch. The spacing changes the appearance of the final pattern.

Notice on the bottom graph, the rows are moved up one thread and over one thread. This maneuver gives a very subtle and gradual diagonal flow.

Stripes, borders, walls, floors

Before every airline flight, I check my purse and carry-on very carefully for any stray scissors. I always ask my husband if he removed his pocket knife. We were boarding one flight, he got checked and rechecked at Security. He had a money clip with a small knife inside! They found it.

After having to mail the clip home twice, I decided the only solution was a new money clip with no knife.

OVERLAPPING CROSS

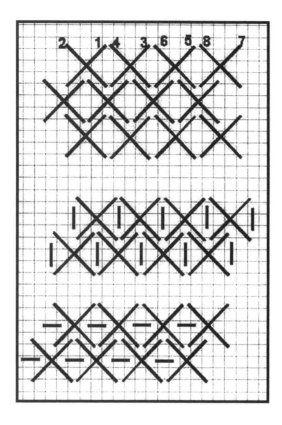

Model 3

The size of the Overlapping Cross Stitch may be changed. The graph also shows a small Gobelin Stitch between the Cross Stitches. The Gobelin Stitch could also be bugle beads or upright crosses. The straight stitches inside the crosses cover the travel threads.

Bushes, clothing, borders, walls

Gerry was working on a quilt. Her friends asked her what her project was. She said it was a baby present. They asked when the baby is due.

"About a year ago! So now it is a first birthday present. I need to get it finished because I am tired of being grounded."

"Grounded?" Her friends asked, astonished.

She said her husband would not take her anywhere until she finished the quilt, and he was tired of being grounded, too!

It worked. The baby got a birthday present for her birthday! Gerry says she won't tell her husband about any more deadlines!

CAESARS

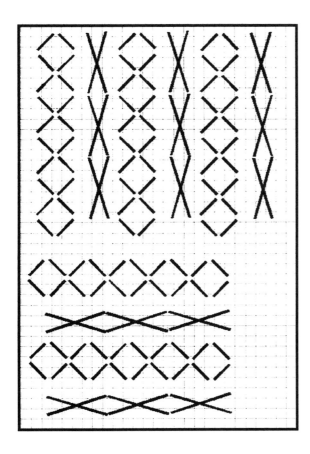

Model 2

Caesars is best worked in rows. The rows may be arranged differently if that is preferable for the area being worked. A couching thread could be placed behind one or both of the patterns.

Wallpaper, dresses, floors, buildings

An impression some people have is that creativity consists of lightning striking them on the head in one great glorious moment. This experience may occur for some people, but usually creativity is the result of hard, persistent work.

Next time you are tempted to throw a piece across the room and never pick it up, remember creativity consists of a great deal of persistence. Another word for persistence is stubbornness.

ELFIN

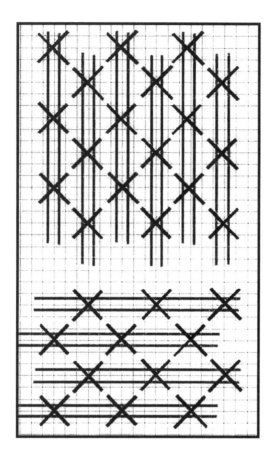

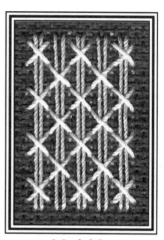

Model 2

Elfin was so named because it made a lovely background for an elf canvas. If one color is used, this is a truly subtle pattern. A metallic thread would give the appearance of stars or snowflakes.

Wallpaper, starry sky, snow, clothing, Santa's sleigh, packages

When you are doing a raised stitch, it is sometimes difficult not to snag it with future stitches. One way to prevent snagging is to baste a piece of tissue paper over the stitched area. Cut the paper to fit the stitch, and baste around the edges. When the rest of the stitching is complete, remove the paper.

WURTH ZIG ZAG

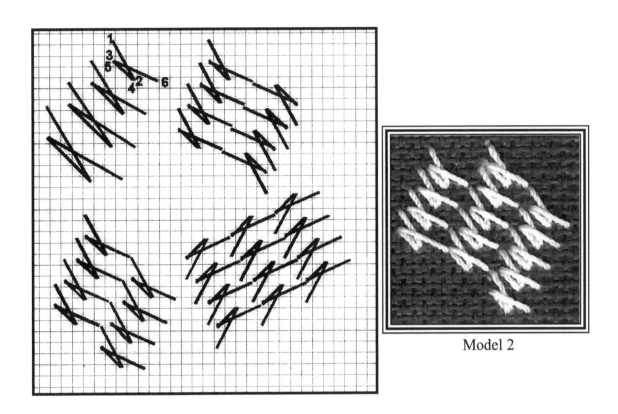

Model 2

Since I found this pattern in one of Jim Wurth's charts, I decided to name if for him. This fun little stitch soon develops a rhythm and can be useful for many areas.

Snow, cuffs, collars, packages, bushes

Some thoughts on personal resource center enhancement, enlargement and further additions:

"More is never enough!"

"The local economy needs me - starting with my needlework shop!"

"There are worse habits than stitching!"

"My friend, the guild, the Internet, or whoever else, made me do it!"

"My stitching friends were getting tired of each other. They needed some new friends!"

OPEN SPRING

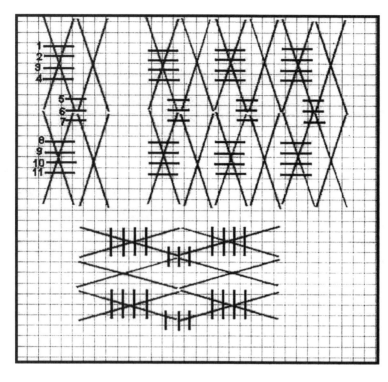

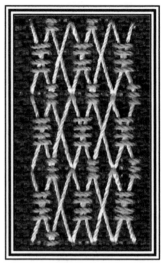

Model 2

Make the cross stitches first and then do the straight stitches over them. Work the straight stitches in rows from top to bottom and then back up. Cover two crosses in each path of the straight stitches.

Wallpaper, floors, curtains, skirts

Just because you buy it does not mean you have to start it, stitch it, or heaven forbid, finish it.

However, if you do finish something, be sure everyone knows that you have actually done a complete project.

DOUBLE CROSS

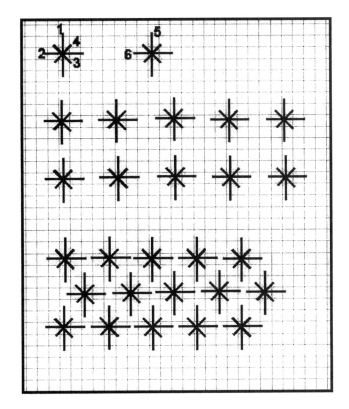

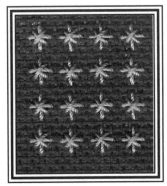

Model 2

Working in vertical rows helps to keep the thread from showing through from the back. Two colors/threads could be used, one for the straight cross, and one for the smaller cross stitches. The upright crosses could be done either first or last, depending on the look you prefer. The graph shows them being done first.

Starry sky, snow, wallpaper, dresses

As far as I know there are no reported cases of people dying from too much housework, laundry or cooking. However, I prefer to take no chances!

I know some people like to cook, and my philosophy is: if they like to cook, I will not deprive them of their pleasure. I assume many of these people work in restaurants, so I am keeping them happy when I eat out!

FRAMED CROSS

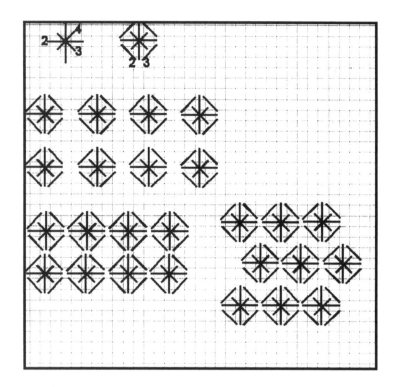

Model 2

The framing stitches are the ones done in metallic which gives a sparkle to the stitch and makes the crosses "pop forward." These stitches do not have to be done in a different thread or color.

In the first example on the graph, working in vertical rows helps keep the thread from showing through. In the second choice, either horizontal or vertical rows are equally acceptable. The third graph one is best worked in diagonal rows.

Starry sky, snow, wallpaper, flowers, bushes

If you are having trouble threading a needle, the first thing to do is to turn the needle around, so you are putting the thread into the other side. Needles are manufactured by pushing a stamp through them, so one side is wider than the other. This process causes one side to be easier to thread.

Another suggestion is to dampen the needle. I did not believe this idea until I tried it, and it works!

BOW TIE

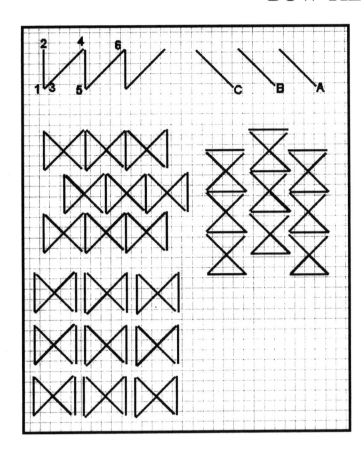

Model 2

Bow Tie is another type of framed cross stitch. Do the stitch in two passes for each row and then move to the next row. If you want to add another color/thread, work the cross stitches first and then the straight stitches.

Borders, stripes, walls

Sometimes there is a project that you have started and never finished for whatever reason. If anyone ever asks about it, try the forgetful approach - theirs, not yours.

"Oh, you must remember, I finished that eons ago and gave it away!"

If pressed, the person you gave it to moved out of the country, died, or is no longer in communication with you.

CROSS STITCHES

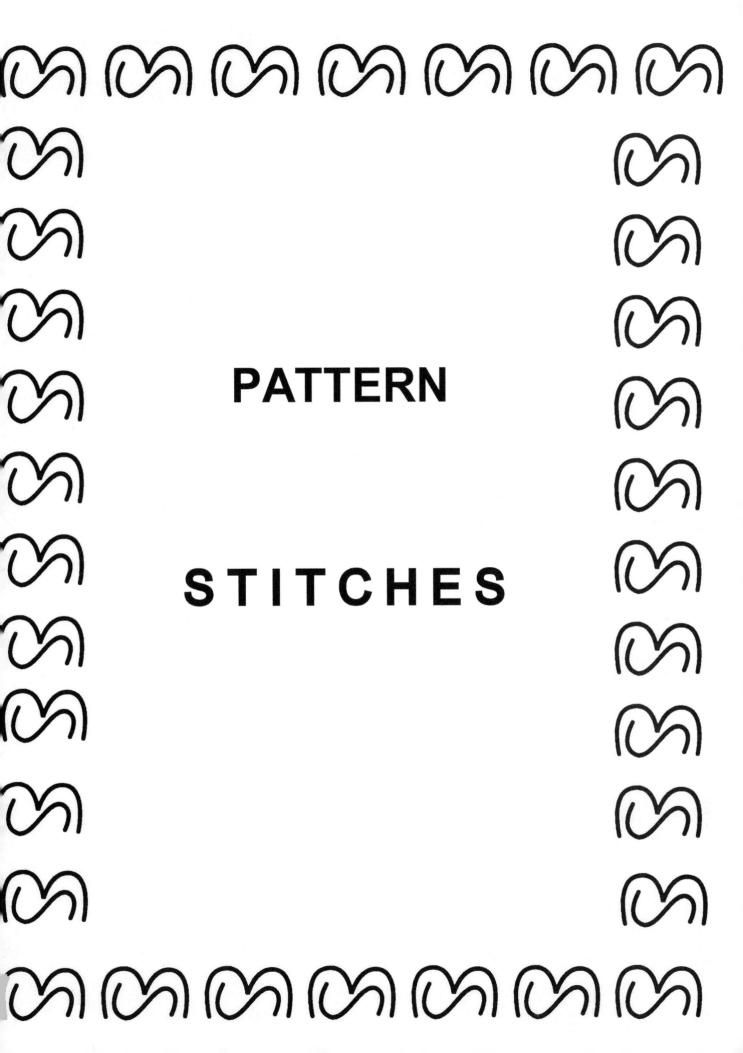

PATTERN

STITCHES

OPEN WAVY A

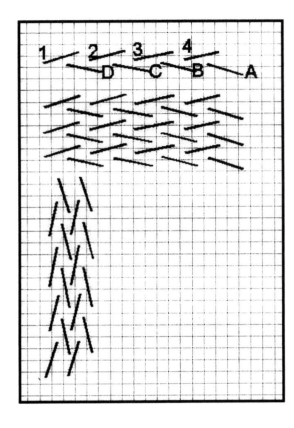

Model 2

The length of Open Wavy stitches can be varied. Longer stitches would give a more open appearance.

Hair, grass, mountains, clothing, water

Sometimes you need to find the center of your canvas when you do not have a ruler. Take two lengths of thread and run them diagonally across your canvas and where they intersect is the center. This technique may be off by a canvas thread or two, but seldom do we need to find the perfect center!

OPEN WAVY B

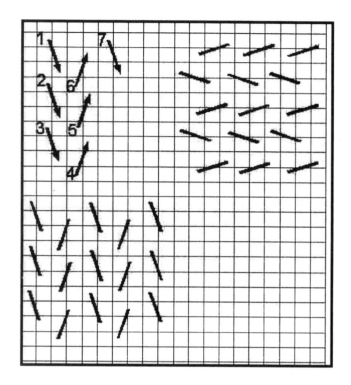

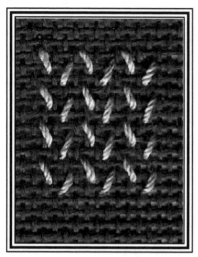

Model 2

A row of canvas between the stitches makes a more open look. The individual stitches can be made longer and there can be even more blank spaces between rows.

Hair, grass, mountains, angel's wings, water

If you are not the fastest stitcher in a class, it is actually an advantage. You can benefit from everyone else's progress. Remember "The early bird catches the mistake!"

Penny is our local 'Turbo Stitcher' and she has learned the lesson the hard way more times than she cares to relate.

However teachers and members of the groups love to have her working with them on projects - it makes their lives much easier!

OPEN WAVY B VARIATION

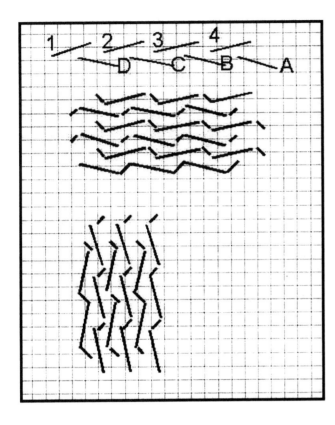

Model 2

The tent stitches are added last. They could also be beads or French Knots. A metallic thread for the tents would be very effective.

The tent stitch could be added to any of the wavy stitches. A more dense pattern is created with the addition of the tent stitch.

Hair, water, grass, clothing, angel's wings

Traveling? Take individual packs of moist towelettes with you. There are also small jars of liquid soap available. You can use either to keep your hands clean while on the road or in the air.

FOUR WAY CONTINENTAL

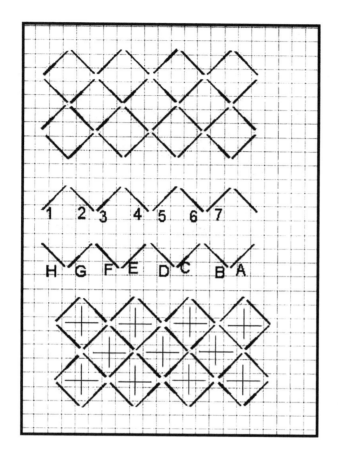

Model 2

Here is a well known stitch that certainly qualifies as one to let the canvas show through. It works up quickly and can be varied many ways. The next few pages show examples of Four Way Variations.

Four Way can be used almost everywhere, so the list below does not begin to exhaust the possibilities.

Snow, sky, flowers, angel's wings

Stitching is not and should not be a competition of any kind. Someone will always be faster or slower than you are. Someone will also stitch better than you and you will stitch better than someone else. The object should be to relax, enjoy yourself and be the best <u>you</u> can be.

FOUR WAY CONTINENTAL A

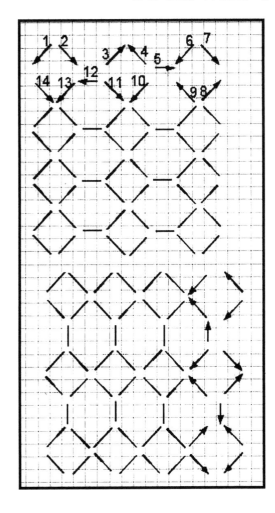

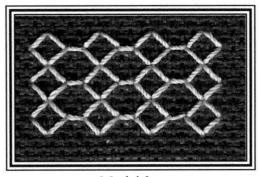

Model 2

Working this Continental Stitch in rows, doing every other straight stitch, keeps the front clean.

Hillsides, clouds, sky

A couple of thoughts to help you achieve perspective on your stitching.
> Small stitches and dark colors recede. The use of fewer strands also causes things to recede.
> Large stitch patterns and light colors come forward.

FOUR WAY CONTINENTAL B

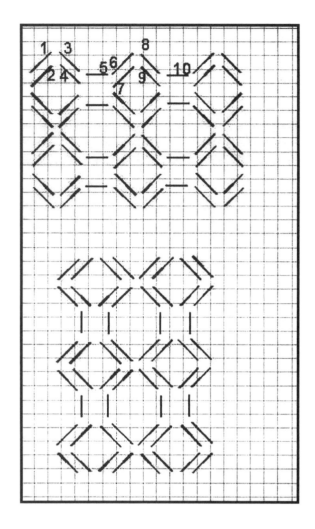

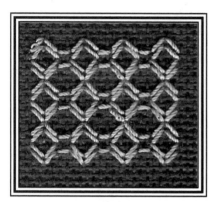

Model 2

Following the count shown on the graph keeps the threads form showing through. Do two parallel diagonals, then the other two diagonals and then the straight stitch. This technique allows you to cover two diamond patterns in two passes.

Wallpaper, floors, borders, pillows

Stitching with a frame or stand not only allows you to lay threads, it also allows you to use both hands. It can make your work move more quickly. Kay has found another advantage to being able to use two hands. She has arthritis, and by rotating the hand on top, it prevents her from making the same motion constantly and aggravating the problem.

FOUR WAY CONTINENTAL C

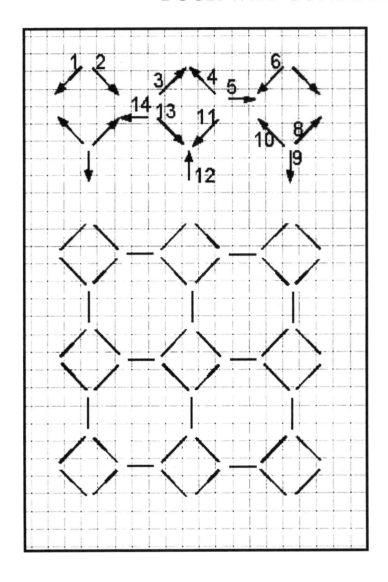

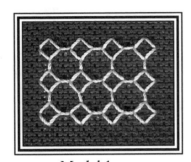

Model 1

The addition of a horizontal Gobelin is what changes this choice from Four Way 1A, making this one somewhat rounder and larger.

Wallpaper, floors, fabric

If you have 'fuzzies' on the top of your work, take a needle threaded with metallic from the front to the back of your canvas. The metallic draws the little ends down into the canvas and out the back.

FOUR WAY CONTINENTAL D

Model 2

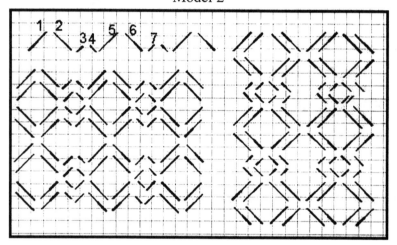

A series of backstitches worked horizontally makes this stitch one of the easiest Four Way Patterns to count. It gives the feeling of intertwined diamonds and has lot of pattern even though it is an open stitch.

Borders, stripes, wallpaper, floors

Every project should have at least three needles. One will get lost in the carpet, one will get lost in the chair and one will just get lost. Needles lost in the carpet can sometimes be found by running a magnet over the area where you think the needle was lost.

Another sure way is to have someone walk barefoot over the area. My husband, however, refuses to participate.

Searching for the needle lost in the chair is a bad idea. You may not find it, but it will find you and that can be very painful!

PENNY

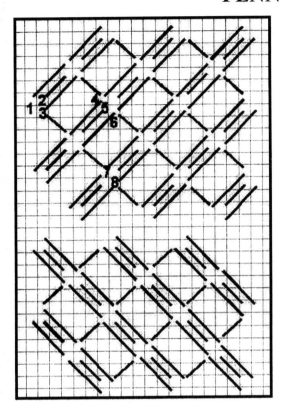

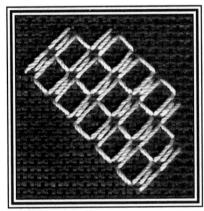

Model 2

Penny can be done in rows because the travel thread will be covered by the diagonal stitch. The diagonal stitch is done last and can be a different color/thread.

Wallpaper, floors, walls

When you are filling an area of canvas with beads, the size of the bead is very important. The following are suggested sizes:

Mill Hill Petite Beads are size 14, their regular beads are size 11.

CANVAS SIZE	BEAD SIZE	SIZE MM
18 Count	14	1.25
14 Count	11	1.33
12 Count	10	1.5
10 Count	8	3
10 Count	6	3.5
7 Count	5	4

FOREST OF TREES

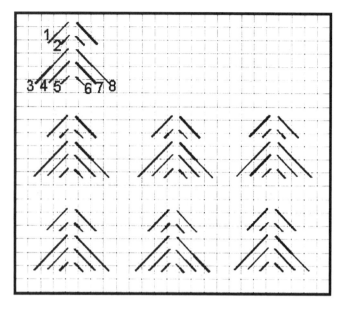

MODEL 3

Work Forest of Trees in vertical rows, doing half the tree at each pass. The trees can be placed as shown, or randomly.

Trees, stripes, borders, Santa's sleigh, clothing, wallpaper

Sometimes odors can become attached to a canvas. Here are several suggestions for removing these odors.

Hang it on a skirt hanger outdoors for a day or two. Simply airing it out may do the trick.

Next spray Febreeze™ in the general vicinity of the back of the canvas - mist it, do not soak it. Then give it a few more days in the fresh air.

You can also try putting it through the home dry-cleaning products - Dryel is one brand.

KITTY

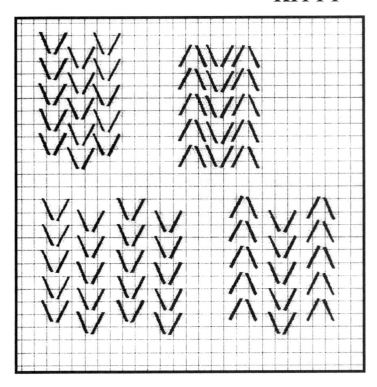

Model 3

Here is a type of open knitting stitch with several variations. It is worked in vertical rows. It can also be turned horizontally. If you worked it vertically for the body of an article of clothing, then you can turn it and work the sleeves horizontally. The size of the individual Vee can be changed.

Fish scales, clothes, snow, clouds, Angel's wings

The husband of a stitcher was asked what he was going to do when he retired. He said that he was unsure since he had no hobbies. It was then suggested that he take up stitching.

He replied that he already knew how to do that. "You go to a needlework shop, buy a whole bunch of stuff, put it into a bag and then, bring it all home and put it in the needlework room."

I think probably many husbands believe this is the case!

DIAMONDS LARGE AND SMALL

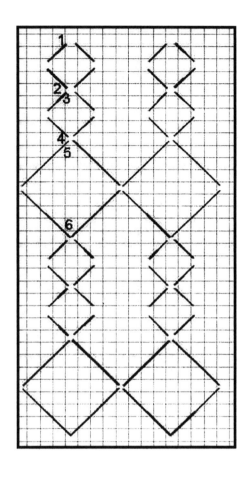

Model 3

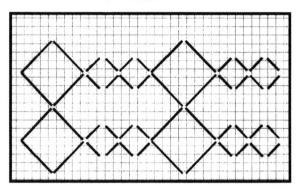

To keep the canvas open, work in rows. Do half of the pattern with each pass. You may chose to have only one small diamond or more of them.

Stripes, borders, wallpaper

If the backs of needlework projects were so terribly important, we would have books and classes devoted to the subject. Some of the titles could be:
"How neat is your backside?"
"Your backside, Tidy, Taut and Trim."
"Your perfect backside - Get it and Show it off."
"Your backside is showing - are you proud?"

DIAMONDS ON A STICK

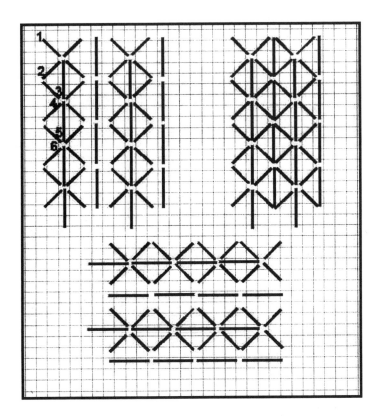

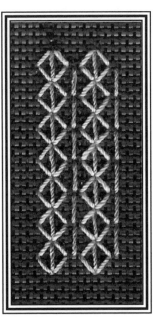

Model 3

Working the diamonds before the straight lines helps keep the lines straighter. The model was done with the straight lines first, and you can see these lines get slightly moved when the diamond is added on top. You can elect to use two colors/threads for this choice.

Stripes, wallpaper, borders, skirts

Have you noticed some of the things that seem to happen overnight when we are sleeping?

The eyes of needles are getting smaller - in fact I have bought some needles that have no eyes at all. The canvas holes are becoming increasingly smaller. Congress cloth used to be a delight to stitch on, but it seems that the manufacturer is losing all quality control.

At the same time, clothes hanging in my closet are getting smaller. The clothing industry also has a problem with quality control. The sizes mean nothing anymore, because a size 10 just keeps getting smaller and smaller.

DIAGONAL BOXES

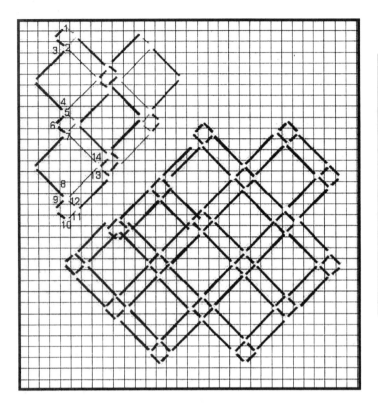

Model 3

This pattern can be somewhat confusing when you first look at it. If you follow the count shown above, and work backstitches in rows, it will become clearer as you go along. This stitch is one you may want to practice on a doodle canvas.

Walls, floors, wallpaper, rugs

I received a frantic email from a friend who was having a frustrating evening attempting to work with rayon threads. She asked me for any advice I might have.
She did figure it was a major breakthrough to be frustrated about something besides her ex son-in-law.

SINGLE DIAGONAL BOXES

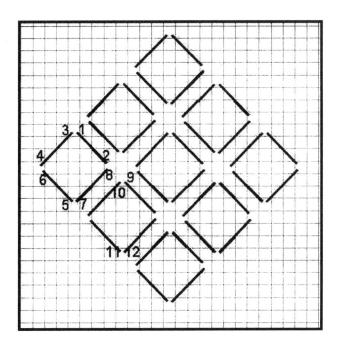

Model 3

The count shows working each box individually and then moving onto the next one diagonally. This pattern would lend itself to being couched before working the diamonds.

Floors, walls, wallpaper, Santa's sleigh

Most stitches can be worked in several different ways. The exceptions to this possibility are Basketweave and open, lite stitches. If you are having trouble working a stitch, look at the graph and see if you can detect a different path to take.

However, with open stitches, you will need to check the path to be sure your travel threads are not showing.

CRISS CROSS HUNGARIAN BOXES

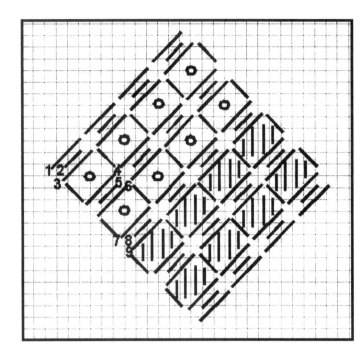

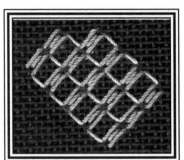

Model 3

Do the sets of three diagonal lines first. By working these diagonal lines as numbered in the graph, when you go back and do the cross lines, they will cover the travel thread. A second color/thread can be used for the cross lines.

The centers can be French Knots, beads, a stitch pattern or left blank as shown on the model. The open appearance of the stitch will vary depending on your choice.

Wallpaper, pillows, quilts, sidewalks

Beverly talked through all sporting events on television. Needless to say this did not please her husband, so he suggested she find a hobby she could pursue when he watched (and listened to) sports. She chose Needlepoint. Now he cannot complain about her personal resource center or her preoccupation with her stitching.

HEXAGONS AND SQUARES

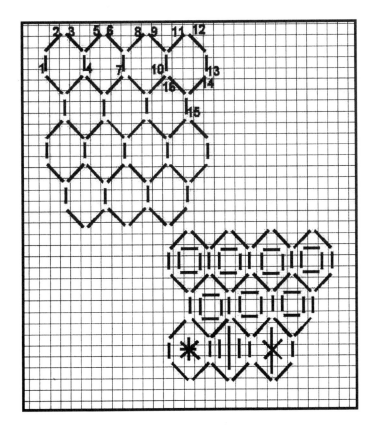

Model 3

Work the diamonds in a series of back stitches, catching the upright stitch on each pass. The centers again offer a variety of choices. I have shown squares, Smyrna Crosses, and Hungarian Stitch. The diamonds can also be filled with beads - Bugle Beads would add a sparkle.

Santa's sleigh, wallpaper, floors, walls, packages

Making beaded fringe that is not tied down can be just the right touch for some canvases. In order to make fringe, bring your needle to the front of the canvas and string the number of beads to form the desired length of the fringe. Then, skipping the last bead (turning bead), go back up through all the other beads and down into the canvas. Go through the first bead again for added security.

For 18 mesh, use #11 beads and a #14 for the turning bead and the fringe will hang nicely.

OCTAGON

Model 3

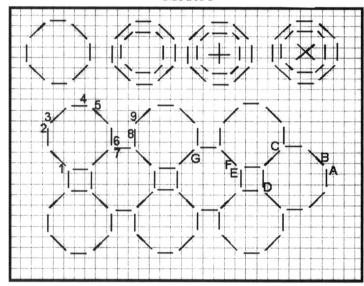

The model is shown open, but there are a couple of options given on the graph if you want more coverage. If you decide to place something inside the Octagon, a second color/thread could be used.

The graph shows the straight horizontal stitch being done on the first pass and the small upright stitches being caught on the second pass.

Wallpaper, clothing, floors, walls

One of the secrets to doing really fluffy looking Turkey Work is to use as many strands as possible and then trim obsessively. When you believe you have trimmed enough, trim at least two more times.

When you are trimming, push a piece of white cardboard under the edge of the Turkey Work. This cardboard helps avoid cutting the stitching around the edges.

SQUARES

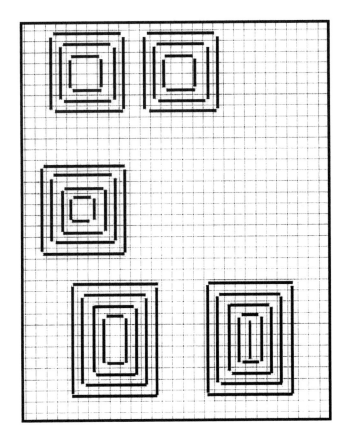

Model 3

Working backstitches around, finish each square completely before moving onto the next one. The size and spacing can be varied as well as the shapes. Again the center can be left open.

Walls, floors, borders, buildings

After you have done all the trimming of your Turkey Work, you have a lot of fluffy fuzz everywhere. You can get rid of the fuzz by using your hair dryer on the cool setting. Canned air can also be found at office supply stores. These are designed to blow the dust from computers but can also be used for blowing fuzz from canvases.

Whichever system you use, doing the job outside seems like a good idea.

SHADOW BOXES

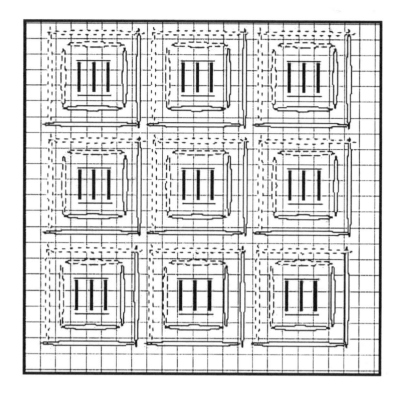

Model 3

The shadow is formed by using three shades of a color. Use the dark color first, then the medium and finish with the lightest. Stitch each box as a unit before moving onto the next box. The spacing of the boxes can be altered. To see the difference the color change makes, look at Model 3 at the back of this book.

Wallpaper, walls, packages, sidewalks, quilts

Rayon threads can be so lovely and add just the right touch to many places, but they can be oh so pesky to use. I have a few suggestions for both the thread and the stitcher.

The thread can be dampened or even ironed. You can also hold it between thumb and forefinger of each hand and give a hard snap or two. This action seems to help control them. Some people find it helpful to double the rayon threads in the needle.

For the stitcher, tension becomes very important - the stitcher's tension, not the threads! Soothing music in the background, a glass of wine at hand and concentrating on keeping the shoulders relaxed. Telling the threads they are beautiful convinces them to behave. However saying this with clenched jaws tends to defeat the relaxed purpose!

SPOOL BOXES

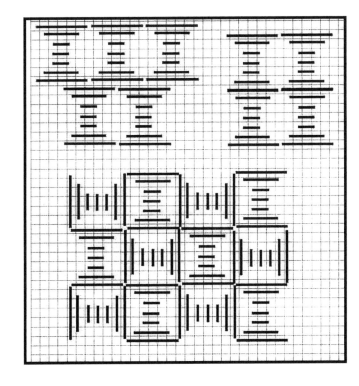

Model 3

Work in rows, completing each spool or box before moving onto the next one. The boxes could also be done with one or more spaces between them.

Wallpaper, walls, sidewalks, packages, quilts

 The other day I went to the basement to look for some knitting yarn. My knitting yarn is in a closet in another room from my needlepoint. I had just opened the closet door, stuck my head in and downstairs came my husband.
I said, "I don't know if you should see this!"
His reply came back immediately, "Oh great, we have a knitting shop to go with our Needlepoint Shop!"
Other than his use of the pronoun 'we' I am afraid he might be very close to the truth!

DIAGONAL CROSS

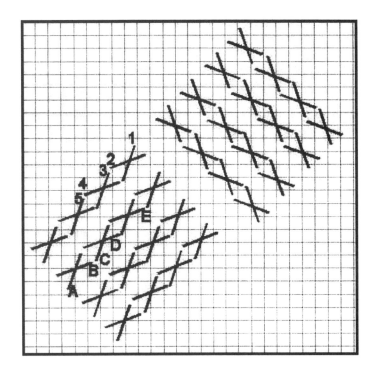

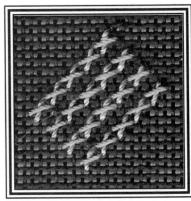

Model 3

Finish each cross before moving onto the next one. The individual crosses can be further apart.

Snow, clothing, packages, Santa's bag

When you are laying long stitches, the first stitch tends to become loose and untidy before you can get the next one laid. Here is a great trick to avoid that. When you have the long stitch in place, hold it with the tip of your laying tool. Then take a backstitch in the next area, only releasing the first stitch when the backstitch is in place. The backstitch holds each long stitch while you proceed to the next one. (The backstitches will be covered by the future stitches).

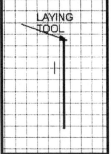

*This tip came from Deborah Wilson of Beau Geste designs.

DIAGONAL ORIENTAL GOBELIN

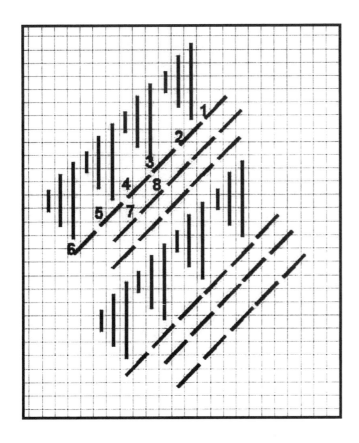

Model 3

The stitches that are numbered are worked as a series of back stitches, going back and forth three times to make those rows. The upright stitches are also worked in rows and can be a second color/thread.

Walls, wallpaper, buildings, hills

The new airport security rules have caused a few problems for stitchers when flying. There are a couple of different cutters available that are allowed. One of these is a Clover Thread Cutter Pendant. I find that it is easier to cut lengths of the threads I will be using and place them in baggies and only have to cut the waste knots when I am actually in the air.

The cutter can be placed on a ribbon or other necklace to prevent loss while in the air. I have worn it around my neck while going through security and never had a problem.

UPRIGHT HUNGARIAN VARIATION

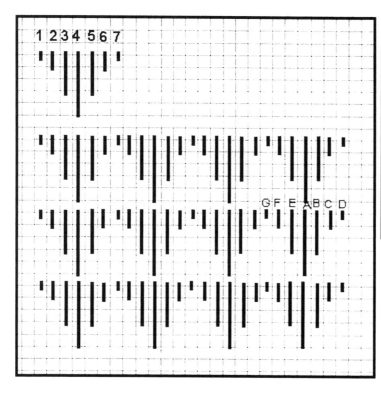

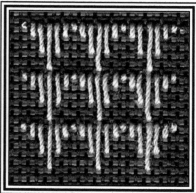

Model 3

In order to move between rows, slide the thread under the stitches and start the second row with a long stitch in the center. Then work out to the edge and back across the row. Look at the second row letters to see the sequence.

Walls, wallpaper, floors, buildings

Another reason to have a large and varied personal resource center is the chance of illness. As I write this book, there is a large flu epidemic. If something like the flu strikes, stitchers need to have several projects available of varying degrees of difficulty. Basketweave might be the best option for such miserable times.

HALF RHODES 4 WAY

Model 3

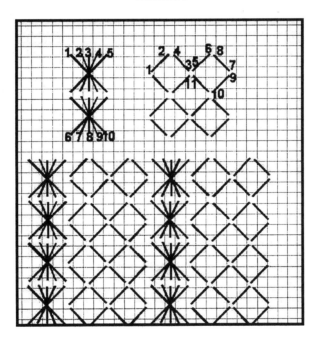

Work the Rhodes Stitches separately from the 4 Way. There can be as many rows of 4 Way as you wish.

Wallpaper, packages, borders, stripes, floors

We use the expression "Four Letter Words" to denote swear words. I would like to add some other words to the usual list - Dust, Cook, Iron, Wash. You notice stitch, sew, needlepoint do not have four letters!

WAVE FILLING

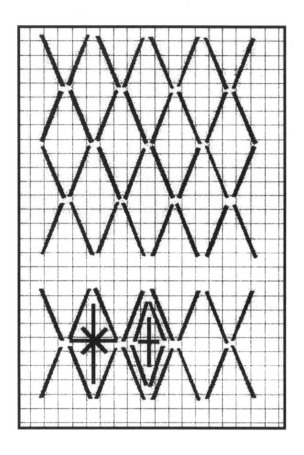 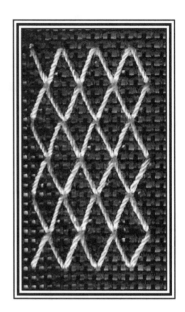

Wave Filling is a fast stitch to work. The size of the crosses can be altered to fit the area you are working on.

Snow, stripes, clothing, borders, quilts, trees

You are never too full for dessert. I have learned it goes into an entirely different stomach than the rest of your food. If, however, you do not feel this is totally reliable, then go for the 'Eat Dessert First' rule of life.

RAY STITCH VARIATION

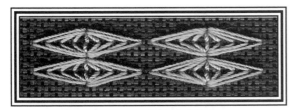

Model 3

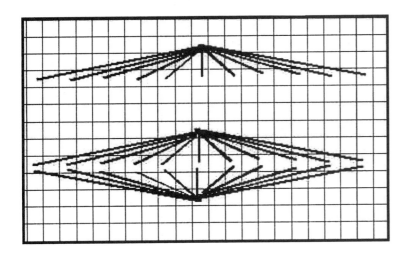

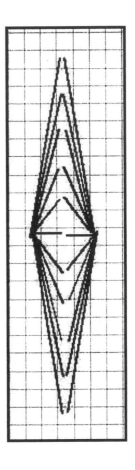

This Ray stitch can be used singly to fill a particular area. If you are doing this, change the count to fit the area. It can also be grouped as shown in the model.

Flowers, bushes, quilts, stripes, borders

Stitch Guides are just that - guides, not commandments. The number of strands suggested may not be the right number for the way you stitch. If you have trouble making the threads look right, try using fewer strands. Sometimes a change in the color of the same thread can make a difference in the way it lays. Using a number different than called for does not make either the stitcher or the writer of the guide wrong - they are just not identical.

OPEN BEAD CUPS

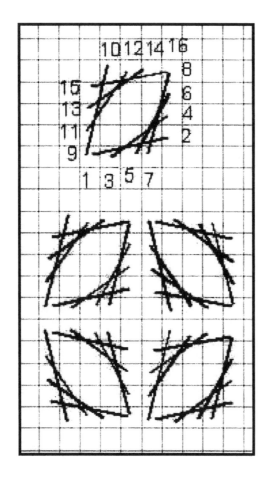

Model 3

Open Bead Cup is actually a Jessica Stitch done on the diagonal. It can be worked as shown or individually. The centers can be filled with beads or French Knots. Grouped together, they form the shape of flowers. A larger bead can be placed between two smaller ones, or two different colors can be used.

Flowers, snow, leaves, borders, quilts

Here are some rules to live by - -
Every outfit needs its own pair of shoes.
Every project needs it own pair of scissors.
If the stitch looks right, it is right. If not, fix it.
If I were not meant to buy something, I would not be where it is!

DIAGONAL WHEAT

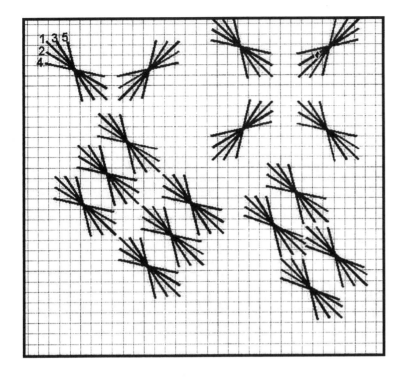

Model 3

The size of the individual stitches can be varied, as can the number of threads between them.

Snow, flowers, fields, curtains

I have gathered several ideas for some of those hard to stitch areas:

Flames - Rachelette or Frosty Rays - Gobelin Stitches
Wood - Pebbly Perle, linen - Stem, Outline, Wrapped Backstitch
Candy Cane - Diagonal Greek, or make a twisted cord and couch onto canvas.
Halos - wrap wire with #16 braid
Snow - Water N Ice - couch irregularly with Snow or braid
Clouds - Freeform Buttonhole or Stem/Outline in rows
Braided Rugs - Work a series of Chain Stitches in a circle.
Gum Drops - Rachel or Flair in heavily padded Satin Stitch
Chocolate - Pebbly Perle

CRISS CROSS HUNGARIAN VARIATION

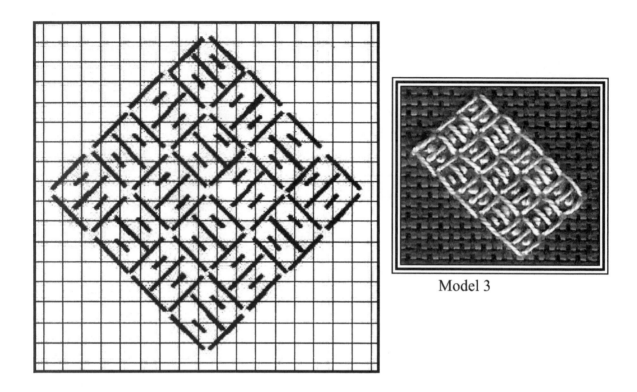

Model 3

Work in diagonal rows. You can do the entire row in one or two passes. If you chose to do them in two passes, do all the diagonals pointing one way on the first pass and the other direction on the second pass. This technique might be easier to start with, until you get the rhythm of the pattern.

Clothing, clouds, wallpaper, packages, Santa's sleigh

Bill sometimes finds it difficult to be enthused to the proper level about his wife's class projects. He claims she spends an entire day in class, and comes home with less than a square inch of the canvas filled.

Kitty then exclaims, "Oh, look what I did! Isn't it just wonderful?"

Bill says that when you have to squint to find the stitched area, it is hard to be as excited as she is.

Now, I do not understand why he finds that so difficult!

GUSSIE'S COUCHING STITCH

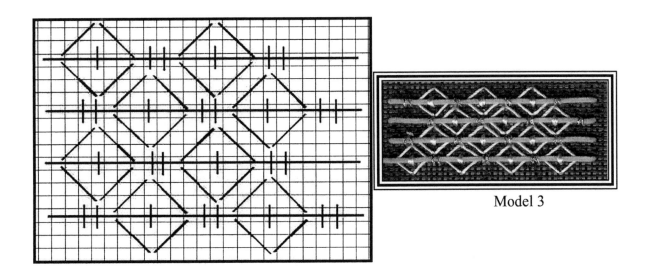

Model 3

This stitch is named for Gussie Schubert of Needlepoint Etc. in Honolulu and the pillow she was making with it. The first layer worked is the four way diagonal stitches. (Note these are over three intersections!) Next the long threads are laid, then the two Gobelin Stitches with which to couch this down. Then do the Gobelin stitches inside the diamonds.

The model starts with the diamonds with Elegance, the long stitches with Very Velvet, the couching stitches are metallic and the last Gobelin Stitches are Neon Rays.

Wallpaper, clothing, furniture, pillows

If for whatever reason, you have a canvas with an odor, you can try freezing it. If the canvas is in plastic, remove it because plastic seems to hold odors longer. A few hours or even days in the freezer should remove the odors. If after removing it, you still can smell an odor, return it to the freezer.

This process can be done even after the piece has been framed.

Freezing works because the cold freezes and thereby kills the spores that are causing the odors. These little guys have attached themselves to your canvas.

What to tell your family about why you are now storing your needlework in the freezer could call for some real creativity and originality. It hardly matters as they won't believe you anyway.

QUODLIBET

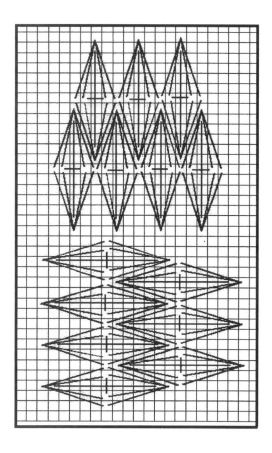

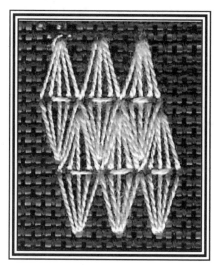

Model 3

I am not sure which is more fun - the stitch or the name. The name is Latin and means "what pleases." A light hearted composition comprising several popular tunes or fragments of tunes ingeniously put together. I don't know how it relates to stitching, but it a fun fact.

Notice the long line is one thread shorter on each end than the slanted lines. They could be the same size, but the stitch seems less bulky this way. The long center line and the cross line can be done first, or last. If first, they tend to sink into the rest of the stitches. They could be in a second color/thread. The cross thread could be eliminated, which makes a less striped look. The second row starts one thread below the row above. The second row could also be spaced two or more threads away if you wanted a more open look.

Clothing, wallpaper, bushes, coconuts

"The only time I ever said no to dessert was when I misunderstood the question." - - Spencer Penrose, founder of the Broadmoor Hotel, Colorado Springs, CO.

STAR

AND

EYELET

STITCHES

OPEN THREE LEGGED CROSS

Model 4

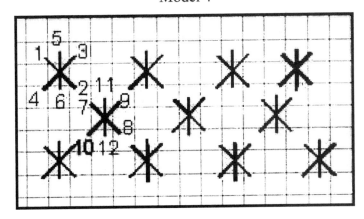

The models show the stitch done two different ways. The Gobelin stitch was done first for the first model (white) and the second model (silver) shows the Gobelin stitch done last. This choice could also be effective with two different colors/threads, one for the cross and one for the straight stitch.

Working in diagonal rows helps keep the thread from showing through.

Starry sky, flowers, dresses, wallpaper, angel's wings

One way to keep random stitches from looking 'thin' is to Basketweave the area first, then add the random stitches on top of the Basketweave foundation. The random stitches can also be done over and over on top of each other. This technique was used on the Elk on the cover of this book.

DOUBLE CROSS GOBELIN

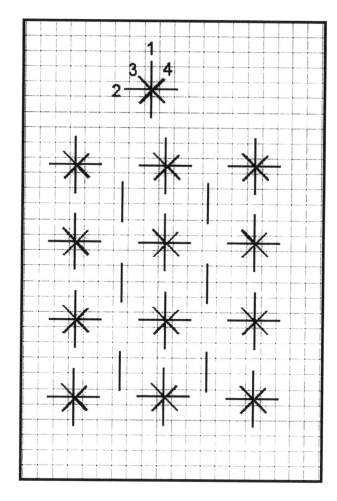

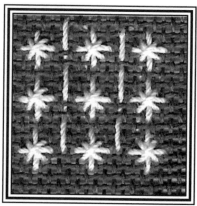

Model 4

The order of working Double Cross Gobelin seems best in vertical rows, doing the crosses and then the straight stitches. Two colors/threads can be used. The rows can also be moved closer together.

Dresses, starry sky, wallpaper, curtains, packages

Fran's husband can see no reason why she needs to own more than one pair of scissors, so she had the store put some away for her. She then told him she left something at the store and came back for the scissors when he was not with her.

DOUBLE CROSS STITCH

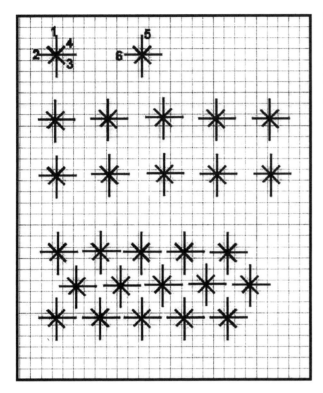

Model 4

Working this Cross Stitch in vertical rows seems the best way to keep the threads from showing.

Starry sky, dresses, flowers, bushes, packages

When there are traveling threads that are not hidden by the stitching, point them out to your framer. Have the piece mounted on the same color as the threads before it is framed. The threads will not show through.

SuZy's Lite Stitches

STARS

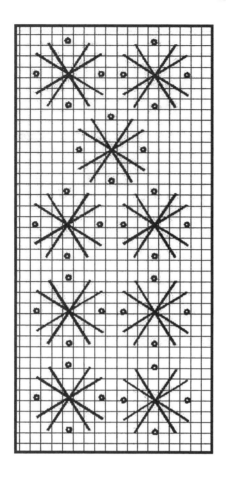

Model 4

The individual stars can be arranged randomly or lined up as shown in the lower part of the graph. The circles can be beads or French Knots. In the model they are French Knots and to make them show up, they were wrapped three times.

Sky, wallpaper, flowers, bushes, clothing, Santa's sleigh

Working on black canvas can be difficult to see at best. You can start by placing a white cloth on your lap, which forms a contrast with the black. You can also get small battery operated lamps that fit onto your lap. This could be called an under light.

Conversely if you are working on a white canvas and having problems seeing, place a dark cloth on your lap.

I have thought of making a sack to carry canvases. One side would be black and the other would be white. So, in addition to carrying the canvas, I would have either color available.

DOUBLE LAYERED CROSS

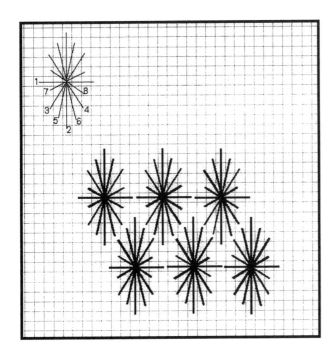

Model 4

This Cross Variation can be done individually or in groups as shown. If the stitches are grouped, then the spacing could be changed.

Starry sky, rugs, clothing, Santa's sleigh

Several ways to know if you are a stitcher:
If your stash of finished and unfinished projects is worth more than your car.
It is 6:00 PM and your planned dinner is still in the freezer, but your stitching is progressing.
You call the needlework shop in a town to get suggestions for motels.
All your computer passwords are stitch related.
You remember all the numbers of the colors you need for your project when you go to the shop,
    but forget to buy shampoo you have needed for a week when you are at the grocery.
You use skeins of thread for picking out paint colors. Then you carry these with you to help you
    remember the color for buying accessories to match the new decor.
No one walks barefoot within several yards of your "stitching nest."
You go to your local shop when you need nothing - "just in case!"
You go to spend the $15 gift certificate you received at the local shop and spend another $100.

TRIPLE CROSS

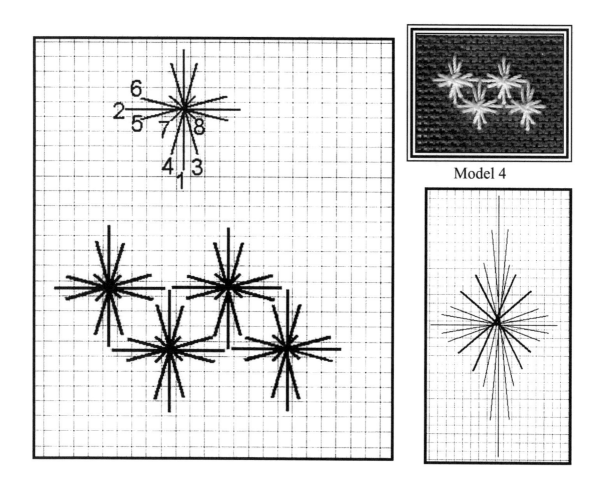

Model 4

Triple Cross is another light and airy stitch. The grouping can be spaced farther apart. The second illustration shows that the lines can be lengthened to make a more dramatic impact.

Starry sky, clothing, Santa's sleigh, rugs

Sometimes there are lines that would cause a jagged effect if stitched in Tent Stitch. The outlines around arms and legs are an example of this type of line. The jaggedness can be eliminated by couching a thread onto these areas. Also an outline or stem stitch can be done. If these don't please, then strand down and use a cross stitch.

BACK STITCHED STAR

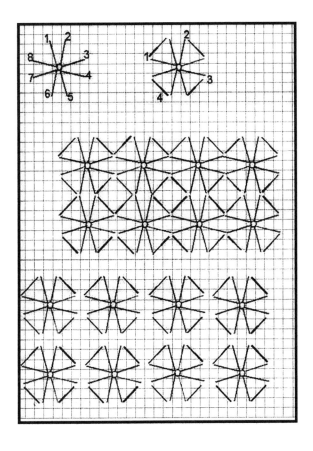

Model 4

Back Stitched Star is a personal favorite. Although the model was stitched using Elegance and Treasure Braid, one color/thread could be very effective.

Rugs, clothing, Santa's sleigh, packages, sky

One of the many satisfying things about Needlepoint is finding the perfect stitch and thread for a particular area. Sometimes the search results in doing something untraditional, so much the better.

If you like the way it appears, then it is a new version of something. Be sure you keep a record of what you did and where you did it.

EYELET STRIPES A

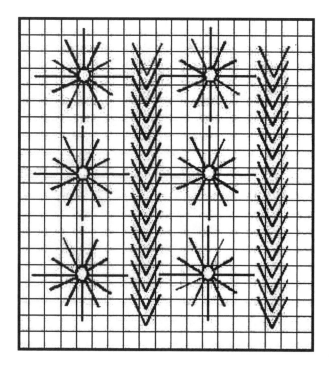

Model 4

Work this pattern in horizontal rows. The Eyelets and the Vee's can be different colors/threads. They can also be spaced farther apart if that fits an area better.

Wallpaper, clothing, rugs, starry sky, Santa's sleigh

One way to avoid traveling threads on the back of Eyelets is to do them ½ at a time. Do one side all the way down the row and then on the next pass, do the other side. This method can be extremely helpful for the Eyelets in this book where there is so much open canvas.

Have a tool handy - the tip of a laying tool is good - to keep opening the eye of the Eyelet, no matter what method you use.

EYELET STRIPE B

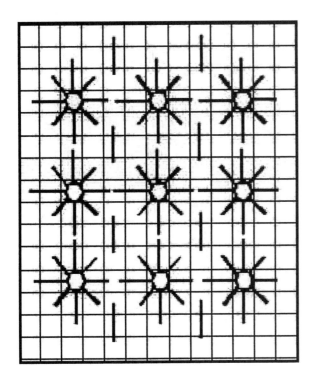

Model 4

Work the eyelets in rows and then come back and work the Back Stitches. The Back Stitches are done with a metallic thread on the model. The metallic gives a nice sparkle to this stitch, but is not necessary. The stitch can also be done with one color/thread.

Clothing, rug, pillows, packages, Santa's sleigh

Another way of working an Eyelet is to do one leg and then alternate. Work every other leg all the way around and then come back and fill in. This method gives a fuller fluffier appearance to the stitch.

Use a tool to keep the center eye enlarged.

EYELET STRIPE C

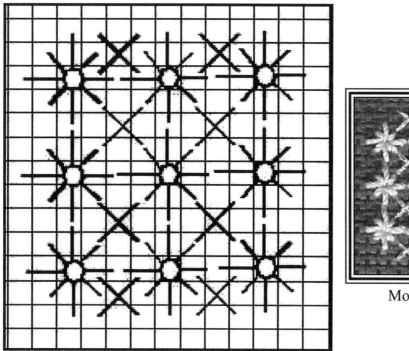

Model 4

The difference here is the addition of the cross stitch. The model was done with metallic. Work in rows, doing the Eyelets first and filling in with the Cross Stitches.

Starry sky, border, flowers, clothing

There are unwritten rules regarding my stitching area - or pit as my husband calls it.

Do not expect home cooked meals, clean clothes or a sparkling clean house when stitching calls.
Do not, under any circumstances, use my scissors.
Do not touch anything, or, even worse, attempt to straighten my mess.
If you find a needle with your bare feet, please return it to its proper place with no complaints.
Do not fiddle with any of the tools in my area. They are not to be considered toys!!!
Do not sit in my stitching chair.

ROUND EYELET

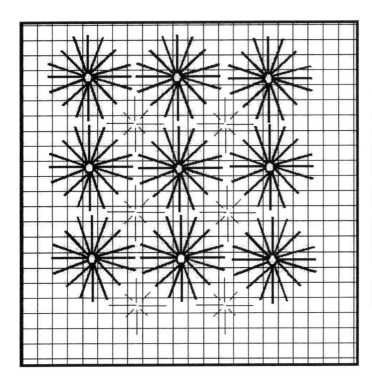

Model 4

The model was stitched using Elegance and Petite Treasure Braid. However, one color/thread could also be used. Round Eyelet gives fairly good coverage, so threads from the back are not much of a problem. I would suggest working in either vertical or horizontal rows.

Snow, clothing, flowers, bushes

An idea for stitching clear areas, such as windows, is to use very sheer organza and stitch it over the area. Cut a piece larger than the area and baste it in place. Trim the fabric close to the basting. Then when you stitch the surrounding areas, you can cover the basting.

When you are working on a project, don't forget to go to the fabric stores and the hobby shops. There is a wealth of things in both of these places that only need your imagination to be placed onto your canvas.

EYELET ROWS

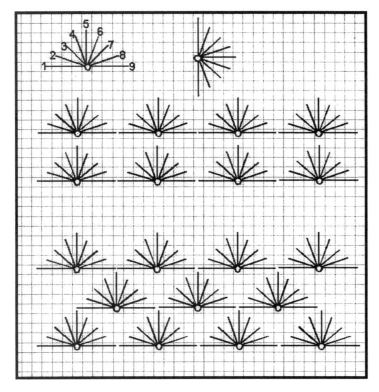

Model 4

The graph shows two different ways of arranging the individual eyelets. They could also be arranged randomly or used singly.

Snow, flowers, packages, wallpaper, borders

I have read that there is a very fine line between Hobby and Mental Illness! If this is true, and I can't imagine that it is, why do mental health professionals recommend people get a hobby to reduce stress? Then the hobby causes more mental illness, so you need to get further help, and be told to get a hobby.

Forget the whole expense of a mental health professional - just spend that money on more needlework supplies! Now if we could only get our health insurance to pay for these supplies, life would be much better.

MINI ALGERIAN EYELET

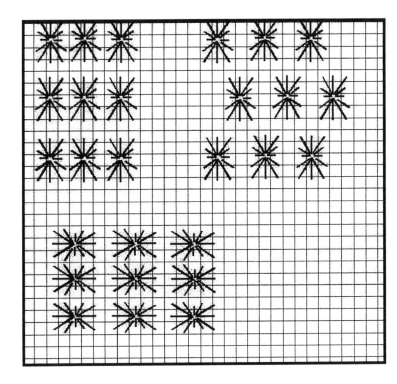

Model 4

The spacing of these eyelets can also be changed according to the area that is being filled. The eyelets can be rotated because they are not the same on all sides.

Clothing, Angel's wings, packages, sky, borders

Every project has three stages:
    "I can't wait to get started!"
        You gather all the threads and they look so inviting, you can hardly stop stitching.
    "I am now stitching and planning. It is so wonderful to see everything develop!"
    "I am almost finished and I am so bored, I can hardly stand to work on the piece anymore!"

Work a little each day. Place your next piece where it is prominent and you can begin thinking and planning.

DIAMOND EYELET AND UPRIGHT CROSS

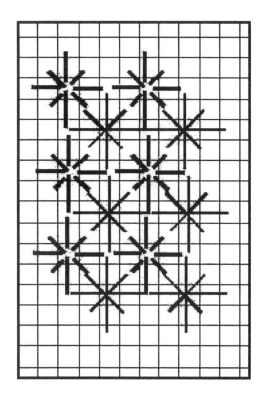

Model 4

The model was stitched using two different threads, but this pattern can be just as effective with one color/thread. The spacing of the individual units can be altered.

Starry sky, dresses, snow, flowers

I know this will come as a shock to many people, but there are no needlepoint police waiting to arrest anyone for breaking the rules. In fact, like painting and music, the rules were meant to be broken. You should understand the reason for the rule in the first place, then you can decide if it applies.

We have so many new threads and embellishment possibilities available now that many of the rules have become obsolete. If a rule has no true basis for existing, then it becomes only a tradition. For instance, not putting small knots on the backs of canvas when we cover the fronts with beads, buttons and bulky stitches.

FULL AND HALF EYELETS

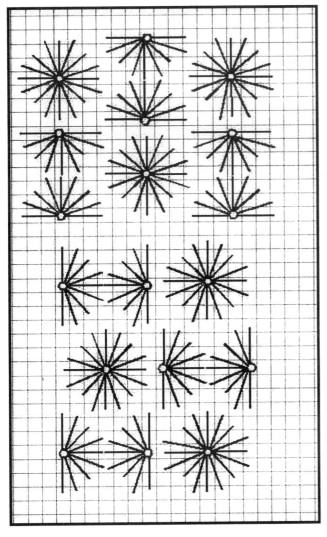

Model 4

These eyelets are so dainty looking. Stitch them in rows, either horizontal or vertical.

Flowers, dresses, wallpaper, packages

If you are having difficulty seeing where to put the needle into the canvas for the next stitch, try turning the canvas over. The path may be easier to see from the back. You can then place the top of a needle into the canvas from the back, turn it over and you will know where to go next.

Looking at the back can also help determine if you have made any mistakes.

EYELETS

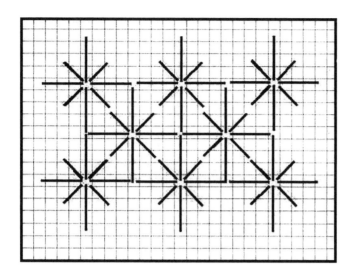

Model 4

The center holes of eyelets can be enlarged. It is a good idea when working them to go through the hole with a larger needle every second or third leg. In order to keep the centers "open," work around and do not cross the center to start another leg.

Sky, dresses, snow, flowers

Speaking of stitching tools. Like all stitchers I had tried diligently to train my children not to tamper, play with, or even touch mine. When my sons got into high school and beyond, I also had to train their friends since our house seemed to be one of the major hang outs. I am not proud to say this process involved some yelling on my part. Of course, I realize the more I yelled, the more fun it became for them to irritate me.

When our older son got married, I gave the groom and John, his best man their own pair of Needlework scissors. The best man was particularly thrilled. He would let no one touch them and spent the week end bragging that he had his own.

John told me he was taking them home, putting them on the table beside his chair and when I came to his house, he would yell at me if I touched them! (I guess he did hear me all those years, after all!)

CRAZY EYELETS

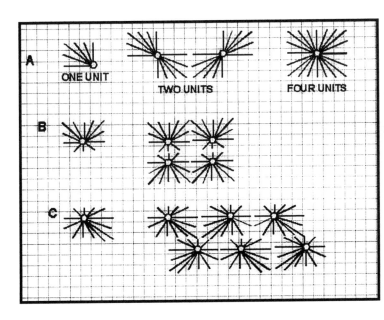

Model 4

Here are just a few of the options you can have with eyelets. By changing one or more of the leg sizes, you can have great variety.

If there is a painted area that is an odd shape, just follow the paint and make a Crazy Eyelet to fit that particular area. There could be many different shapes in one area - stars and snowflakes are just two possibilities.

Stars, Snow, collars, dresses, flowers

When using a waste knot, sometimes it is hard to get the knot cut off without leaving a small amount of thread on the top of the canvas. One way to help avoid this is to tug the knot up and away from the canvas and then cut it off. When you let go, it falls back into the hole and is lost.

There are also curved scissors available that will let you get right up next to the canvas. Now that is specialization - scissors for waste knots. Of course, you need a pair for regular threads and another pair for metallic threads!

EYELET VARIATIONS

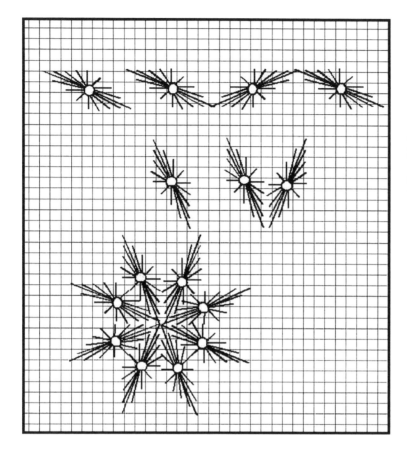

Model 4

The computer is responsible for this pattern. It just kept turning the Eyelets to make up a big circle. The model is stitched with Petite Treasure Braid. This eyelet can be done in groups or individually.

Flowers, packages, individual motifs

Many stitches have delightful patterns formed by the way the individual stitches fit together. Remember, however, that pattern can sometimes be lost when using a dark color thread. If the pattern doesn't show, then it is probably not a good use of a particular stitch. Save the stitch for an area where it can show off its beauty!

OCTAGONAL EYELET VARIATIONS

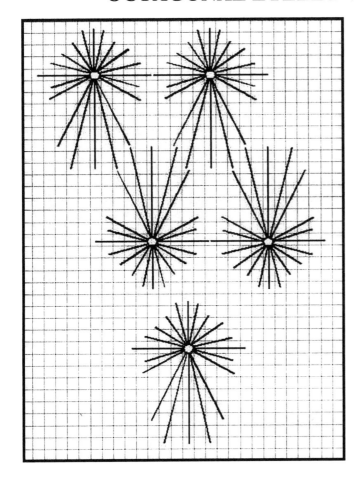

Model 4

Here is another example of eyelets with varying leg sizes. This eyelet is probably best used as a single random motif.

Flowers, borders, wallpaper, individual motifs

If you are having trouble seeing where to put the needle next, stitch with an empty needle. Take a larger needle, and go along the path of the stitch, enlarging the holes slightly. When you have thread in place, the larger holes are easier to see.

(I developed this idea while trying to do four Amadeus Stitches. After I had taken them out enough times, the larger holes made it faster and easier to see where I should be going!)

BUTTONHOLE EYELET

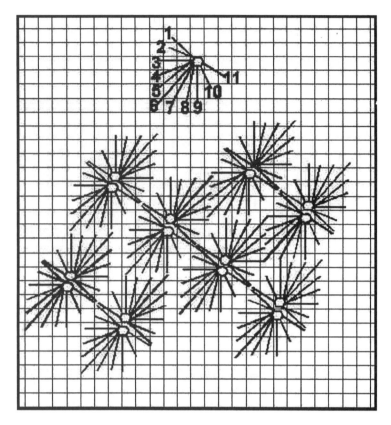

Model 4

Do half the row of Eyelets and then come back and do the second half. These stitches are best done with one color/thread. A lighter thread would give a really delicate appearance to an area.

Flowers, starry sky, clothing, individual motifs

Fuzzy threads are more effective in long stitches. If you brush the stitches after they are in place, an irregular stitch is fine. Again the pattern won't show. These threads can also be couched. If they are not going through the canvas holes, lay them onto the front of the canvas and couch them in place with a finer thread. These couching stitches can be done almost invisibly, or they can become part of the pattern by using a contrasting thread.

TRIANGULAR EYELET

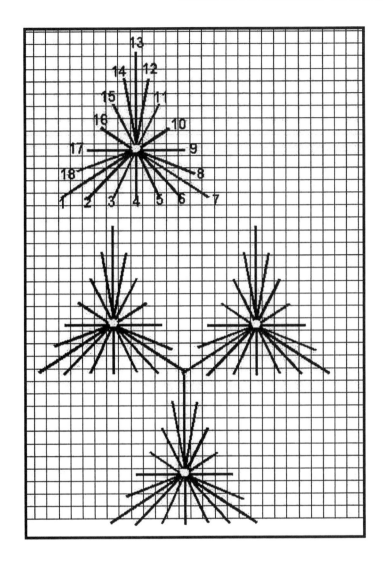

Model 4

Work this stitch in rows. The spacing shown is only one possibility. Consider using one of these stitches as an embellishment on a fancy dress or sky.

Flowers, borders, individual motifs

If a flat thread, such as a ribbon, is not laying correctly on the front of the canvas, turn the canvas over and straighten it on the back. Sometimes flat threads need to be laid on both the front and back of a canvas.

TRIANGULAR EYELET VARIATIONS

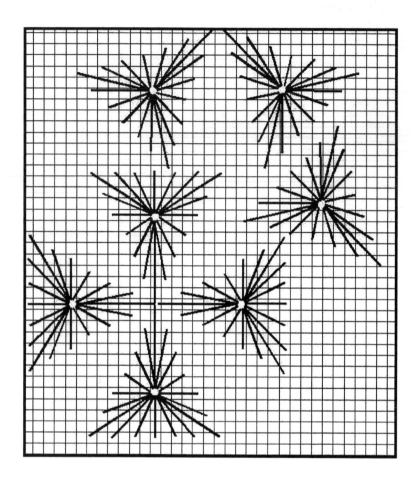

This illustration shows how the same stitch can be turned several ways and form a larger motif.

Flowers, borders, wallpaper, individual motifs

When you are having trouble getting a thread through the canvas, try a larger needle. This approach seems backwards, but the larger eye enlarges the opening and makes it easier for the thread to go through.

EYELET VARIATIONS

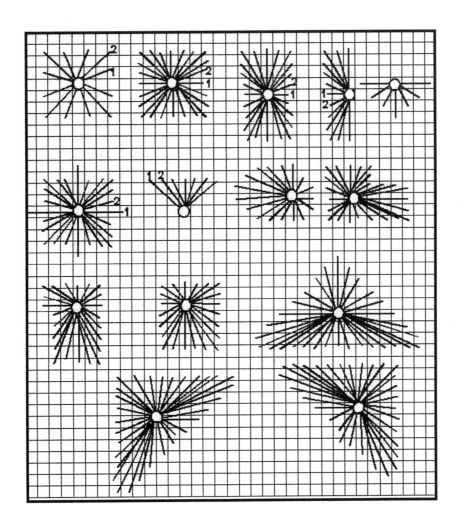

This page just proves "Eyelets are like potato chips." I could not graph just one, once I got started they just kept coming.

Flowers, borders, wallpaper, individual motifs

Basketweave is sometimes the only stitch that will fit an area. It also gives the eye a place to rest, which is important for any canvas.

There are also times when Basketweave is the best stitch for the way you are feeling either emotionally or physically. The rhythmic monotony of the stitch can be soothing, especially during times of stress.

STARS

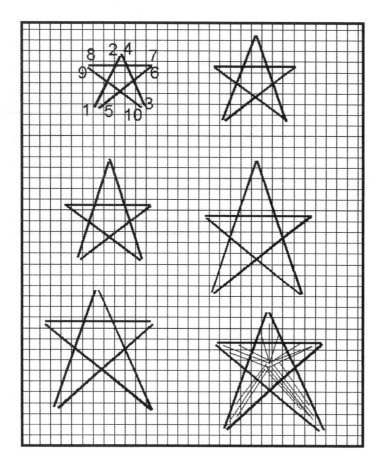

Model 4

Joan Lohr shared these ideas with me as possibilities for the stars found on many painted canvases. These stars show a few of the possible sizes, which can be filled in to match the paint. They could be left empty, as shown in the model, filled in with Tent Stitch, or filled in with lines as shown in the bottom graph.

Stars

Flair and Rachel are delightful threads that can tend to fray. Cut them at a sharp angle and apply Fray Check™ to the edges. If they begin to fray in spite of these precautions, cut them again immediately.

The tension of these threads can be changed to create different appearances. If you use a long stitch and do not pull them tight, let them puff up and fill an area. Experiment with different tensions to see how their appearance changes.

SCRUNCHIES

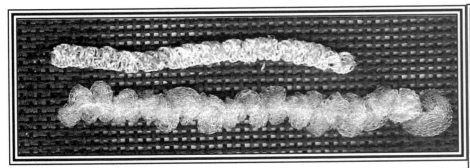

The two examples on the top are done with Frosty Rays. The left one is just pulled through, while the right one has been shaped slightly.

The long one on top is Sparkle Rays and the bottom one is Frosty Rays. These unique stitches can be done long or short, shaped or not. The amount of gathering can also be changed.

This stitch is more of a process than a stitch.

Cut a length of Rachelette, Frosty Rays or Petite Frosty Rays and attach to the canvas. Bring the thread to the front and holding the center thread only, gently pull the outside down to the canvas. Then take the center thread to the back and pull as snugly as you want. Secure this thread and you have a scrunchie.

You can also use Flair or Rachel, with a gathering thread run through it.

Sparkle Rays can also be used for Scrunchies by separating one thread from the others and again gently pulling. Gussie used this method for a trim around a pillow that was drawn onto the canvas.

Fake Bullions can also be made with Silk N Ivory, Trebizond, Silk Serica by pulling one thread and let the others form a "Curl."

Some canvases have some areas that are not easily identified. The technical term for these areas is 'blobs!' Scrunchies can be applied to these areas and they look wonderful. Several of them can be placed in a group to form flowers.

Pat was the first one in a class to make a Scrunchie. When she pulled the center thread and watched the Flair part do its thing, she emitted a sound that was a cross between a squeal and a squeak. No one was quite sure what it meant, but she said it was a sound of approval.

*The ladies of Hawaii had to wait until the very end of the book to get their favorite stitch!

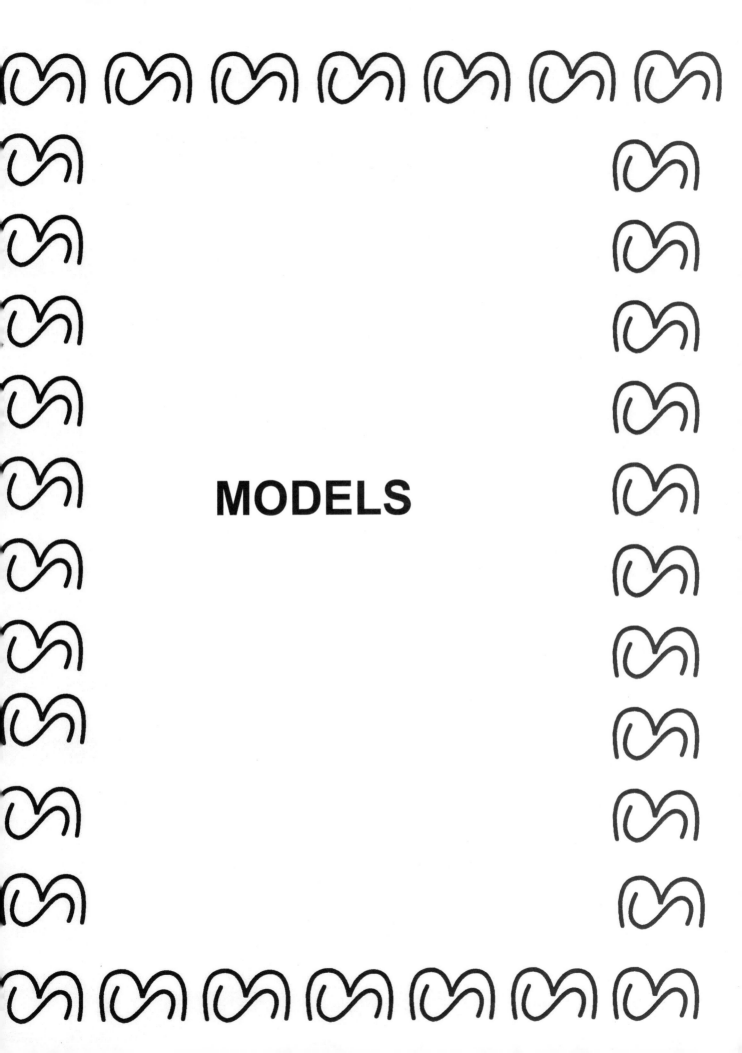

MODELS

ELK by Liz

ELK BY LIZ

MALE ELK
> Brown Medici - #8500, 8841
>> Tent stitch his legs and head. Encroaching Gobelin over two canvas threads for his body.

FEMALE ELK
> Brown Medici - 8838, 8839, 8840
>> Tent stitch her entire body.

ANTLERS
> Petite Very Velvet, V606, V608, V609 - Tent Stitch

SKY
> Random long and short with one ply of Needle Necessities Overdye Floss # 185

TOP CENTER MOUNTAIN
> Using one strand of Anchor Floss #234 and one strand of Accentuate #300,
> work Bargello, following the line of the mountain . Go over four threads for the first row,
> then over two and continue this pattern.

RIGHT TOP MOUNTAIN
> With Rainbow HiLights #607, work Double Twill Stitch over 4, skip
> one thread, go over 1 thread and then repeat.

CENTER RIGHT MOUNTAIN
> Two strands of Anchor #398 for the long stitches and one Balger #8
> Braid #025 for the short ones.

LEFT MOUNTAIN
> DMC Floss - #413, 414, and 318. #8 Balger Braid #025.
> Changing colors as you work down the mountain, use the metallic
> for the tiny stitches

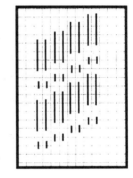

BOTTOM OF THE MOUNTAINS
> Overdye Floss #173 - 2 ply,
>> Double Hungarian

TREES
> Accentuate #300- 1 strand
>> Brick over 4 threads.

SNOW
> #8 Balger Braid #100 - White
> Horizontal Parisian

ROCKS
> Overdye #1281 - 4 strands - Gobelin over the area.

TWIGS
> Overdye Floss #125 - Brown, 2 strands - Stem Stitch

RIVER ICE
> Nordic Gold ND17 - Random long stitches.
Brush both Elk when all the stitching is completed.

SuZy's Lite Stitches

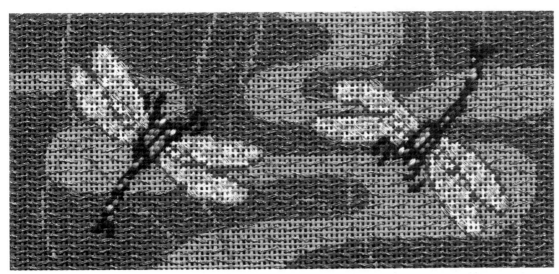

Dragon Flies by Lee's Needle Art
Stitched by Kitty Moeller

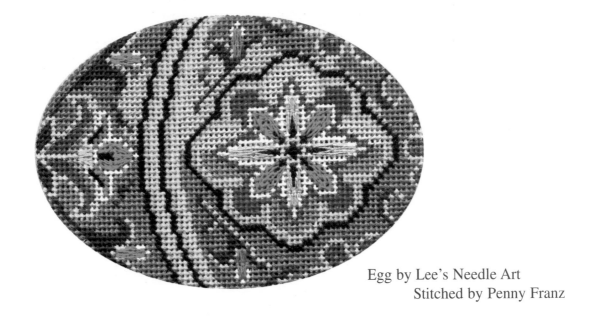

Egg by Lee's Needle Art
Stitched by Penny Franz

Pansies by Lee's Needle Art
Stitched by SuZy Murphy

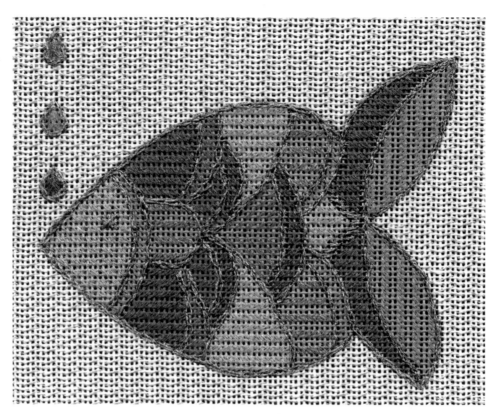

Fish by Sharon G
Stitched by SuZy Murphy

Ornament by A Collection of Designs
Stitched by Connie Wise

Peonies by DeDe's
Stitched by Penny Franz

Enchanted Santa by Liz
Stitched by SuZy Murphy

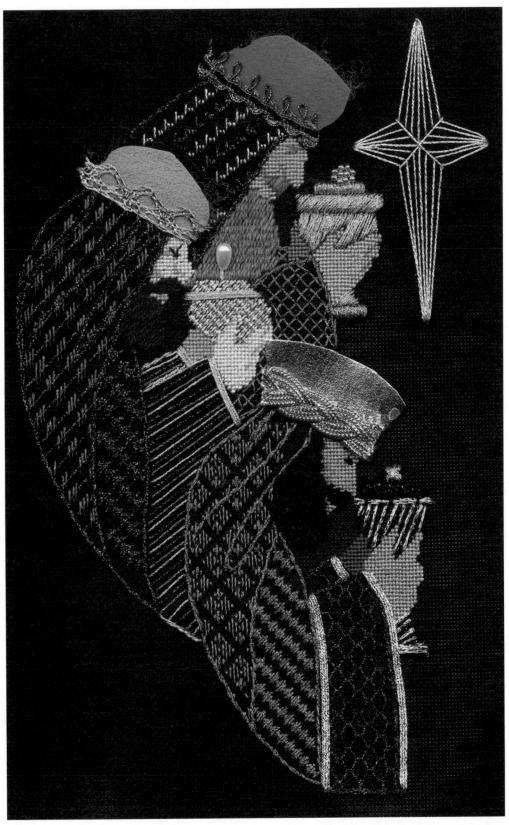

The Magi by Sandra Maag Reddell
Stitched by SuZy Murphy

MODEL 1

WOVEN PATTERN	OPEN ZIG ZAG	STRAIGHT MOSAIC VARIATION A	STRAIGHT MOSAIC VARIATION B	STRAIGHT MOSAIC VARIATION C	OPEN GOBELIN	STAIR STEPS
STAIR STEPS	OPEN STRAIGHT ORIENTAL	MILANESE VARIATION	MINI DIAMONDS	GOBELIN BY 3		
OPEN TWILL	PILLARS	ROLLING ARROWS	BENJAMIN			
LANTERNS	COUCHING PATTERN A	COUCHING PATTERN B	COUCHING PATTERN C	BRICK COUCHING		
ARISTEIA A	ARISTEIA B	RAILWAY TRACKS	RAILROAD BACKGROUND			
HUNGARIAN BARGELLO A	VERTICAL WAVE	DIAGONAL HUNGARIAN	HORIZONTAL WAVES	OPEN VICTORIAN STEP		
HUNGARIAN BARGELLO B	TRIPLETS		ELK MOUNTAIN ___ WAVES			

MODEL 2

DIAGONAL WEAVE	PLAITED STITCH	TRELLIS STITCH	DIAGONAL GOBELIN	MOSAIC VARIATION A
MOSAIC VARIATION B	MOSAIC VARIATION C	OPEN SERENDIPITY	DIAGONAL SCOTCH VARIATION	OPEN ORIENTAL
NICOLE A	NICOLE B	NICOLE C	DROPPED MOSAIC	LARGE WOVEN
CRAZY CROSS A	CRAZY CROSS B	OBLONG CROSS VARIATION A	OBLONG CROSS VARIATION B	GOBELIN CROSS A / GOBELIN CROSS B
CROSS VARIATION A	CROSS VARIATION B	ENTWINED CROSS	CAESARS	ELFIN / WURTH ZIG ZAG
OPEN SPRING	DOUBLE CROSS	FRAMED CROSS	BOW TIE	OPEN WAVY A / OPEN WAVY B
OPEN WAVY B VARIATION	FOUR WAY	FOUR WAY VARIATION A	FOUR WAY VARIATION B	PENNY
FOUR WAY VARIATION C	FOUR WAY VARIATION D			

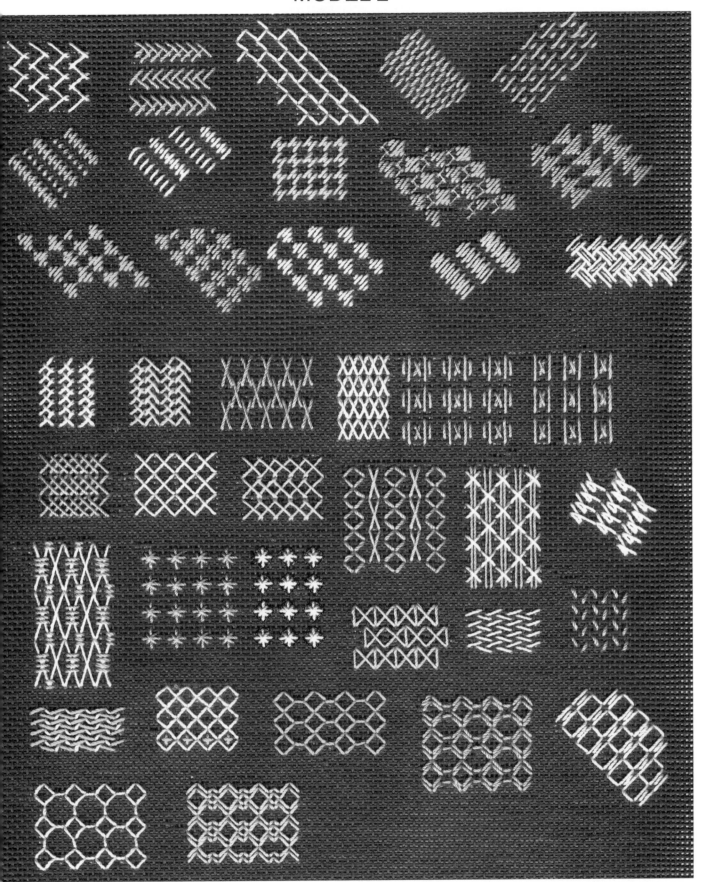

MODEL 3

FOREST OF TREES	KITTY	DIAMONDS LARGE & SMALL	DIAMONDS ON A STICK	DIAGONAL BOXES	COUCHED BOXES
CRISS CROSS HUNGARIAN BOXES					
HEXAGONS AND SQUARES	OCTAGON	SQUARES	SHADOW BOXES	SPOOL BOXES	
DIAGONAL CROSS	DIAGONAL ORIENTAL GOBELIN	UPRIGHT HUNGARIAN VARIATION	HALF RHODES FOUR WAY	OVERLAPPING CROSS	
WAVE FILLING	RAY STITCH VARIATION	OPEN BEAD CUPS	DIAGONAL WHEAT	CRISS CROSS HUNGARIAN VARIATION	
GUSSIE	QUODLIBET				

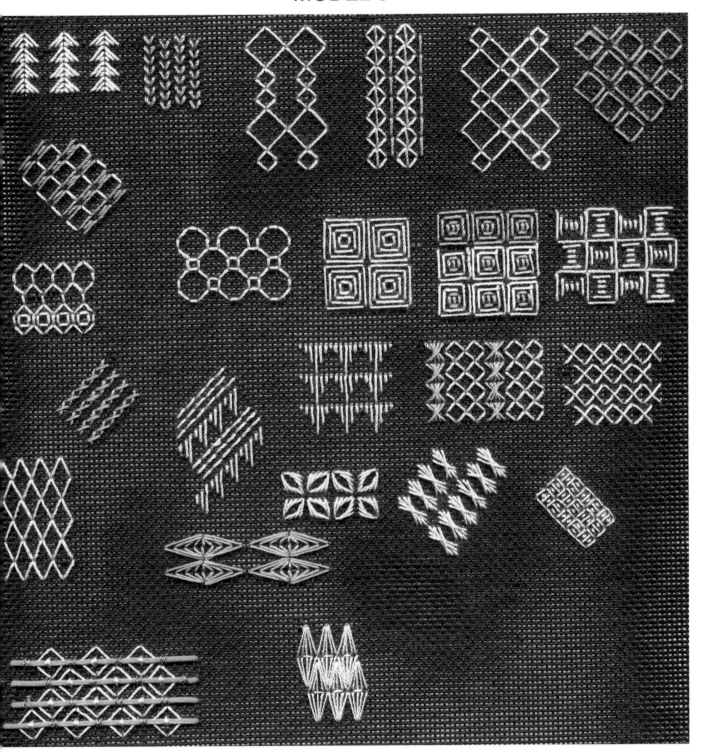

MODEL 4

OPEN 3 LEGGED CROSS	OPEN 3 LEGGED CROSS A	DOUBLE CROSS GOBELIN	DOUBLE CROSS	STARS	DOUBLE LAYERE CROSS
TRIPLE CROSS	BACK STITCHED STAR	EYELET STRIPE A	EYELET STRIPE B		EYELET STRIPE C
ROUND EYELET	EYELET ROWS	MINI ALGERIAN EYELET	DIAMOND EYELET UPRIGHT CROSS		FULL AND HALF EYELETS
EYELETS	CRAZY EYELETS A B C	EYELET VARIATIONS	OCTAGONAL EYELET VARIATION		
BUTTONHOLE EYELETS		TRIANGULAR EYELETS	STAR		

SCRUNCHIES

MODEL 4

STITCH INDEX

EFFECTS INDEX

BIBLIOGRAPHY

American Needlepoint Guild. *ANG Stitch Book 2003*

Bunger, Amy. *Amy's Cookbook for Stitchers,* Memphis, TN. Self Published.

English, Mindy. *The Canvas Embroidery Notebook: Backgrounds,* Atlanta, GA. Self Published, 1992.

Ettl, Susan. *My Canvas Embroidery Notebook,* Green Valley, AZ. Self Published, 2003

Hart, Brenda. *A Banner Year,* Phoenix, AZ. Self Published. 2002

Hart, Brenda. *Favorite Stitches, Book 11,* Tuscon, AZ. Self Published, 1996

Hart Brenda. *Stitches for the Millennium,* Tuscon, AZ. Self Published, 1999.

Hilton, Jean. *Turnberry Ridge.* Self Published, 2001.

Lake, Carole. *Canvas Stitch Notebook,* Self Published.

Lantz, Sherlee and Maggie Lane. *A Pageant of Pattern for Needlepoint Canvas,* New York, NY. Grossett & Dunlap, 1977.

Strite-Kurz, Ann. *Backgrounds, The Finishing Touch,* Midland, MI. Self Published, 2003

Thomas, Mary. *Dictionary of Embroidery Stitches,* Oriental Press Dubal U.A.E. 1998.

Zimmerman, Jane D. *The Canvas Work Encyclopedia,* Richmond, AZ. Self Published, 1989.